COVENTRY TO LEICESTER

via Nuneaton and South to Rugby

Vic Mitchell and Keith Smith

MP Middleton Press

Front cover: No. 66017 passes over the A444 roundabout south of Nuneaton on 30th June 2015. It is hauling the 09.15 container train from Manchester Trafford Park to Southampton Western Docks. (J.Whitehouse)

Back cover: Railway Clearing House map for 1947.

Published January 2017

ISBN 978 1 910356 00 5

© Middleton Press, 2017

Senior Designer Deborah Esher
Typesetting & design Cassandra Morgan
Cover design Matthew Esher

Published by
   Middleton Press
   Easebourne Lane
   Midhurst
   West Sussex
   GU29 9AZ
Tel: 01730 813169
Email: info@middletonpress.co.uk
www.middletonpress.co.uk

Printed and bound by CPI Group (UK) Ltd, Croydon, CR0 4YY

CONTENTS

INDEX

ACKNOWLEDGEMENTS

We are very grateful for the assistance received from many of those mentioned in the credits, also from A.J.Castledine, G.Croughton, G.Gartside, S.C.Jenkins, N.Langridge, B.Lewis, J.P.McCrickard, J.Nash, Mr D. and Dr S. Salter, T.Walsh, and in particular our always supportive families.

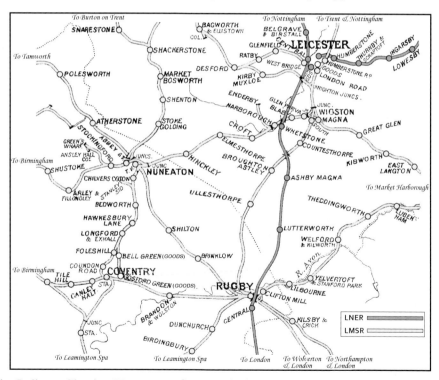

I.   The Railway Clearing House map for 1947 includes the Coventry Avoiding Line, serving Bell Green and Gosford Green. These were goods depots, with cranes rated at 5 and 10 tons. They opened in 1914 and closed in 1984 and 1963 respectively. Between them was a siding for Morris Motors. Another for Chrysler cars became a container depot for Freightliners Ltd. The former's car parts were also conveyed to their factory at Linwood in Renfrewshire. This traffic began on 8th August 1977.

GEOGRAPHICAL SETTING

Most of both routes traversed Leicestershire, but the Rugby and Coventry-Nuneaton sections were in Warwickshire.

The geology around Nuneaton is varied, but the area between there, Leicester and Rugby is predominantly on limestone. North of Coventry there are vast coal deposits.

The district in the north is drained by the River Soar, which flows north into the River Trent. The southern part is served by the tributaries of the south-flowing River Avon, notably the River Swift north of Rugby.

The Roman Fosse Way virtually bisected the triangle later created by the railways, our two routes forming the east and west sides. Industries grew greatly in the three principal towns of this volume, but agriculture generated most traffic in the rural areas between them. The exceptions were the quarries west and north of Narborough, where granite was produced from early igneous activity.

The maps are to the scale of 25ins to 1 mile, with north at the top, unless otherwise indicated.

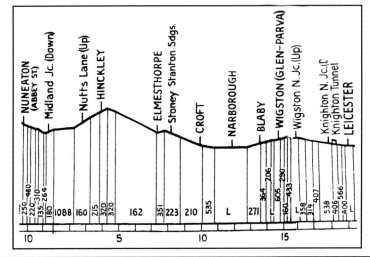

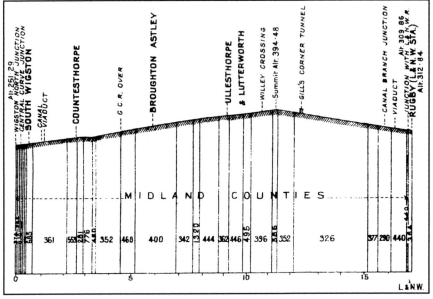

HISTORICAL BACKGROUND

The first main line in the district was that of the London & Birmingham Railway, which reached both Rugby and Coventry in 1838. It became part of the London & North Western Railway in 1846.

Looking at developments southwards, we find the L&BR opening from Coventry to Leamington in 1844 and the LNWR running from Rugby to Leamington in 1851.

The LNWR opened from Rugby to Nuneaton and on to Tamworth in 1847 and from Coventry to Nuneaton on 12th September 1850. The Midland Railway arrived in Nuneaton from Birmingham in 1864.

The South Leicestershire Railway opened between Nuneaton and Hinckley on 1st January 1862 and on to Wigston Junction on 1st January 1864, trains continuing north from here to Leicester over the 1840 lines of the Midland Counties Railway from Rugby. This became part of the MR in 1844 and the route features in the second part of this volume.

North of Leicester, the MCR continued to Loughborough, also in 1840. The MR reached Wigston from Market Harborough in 1857.

The LNWR and the MR both became major constituents of the London Midland & Scottish Railway, upon its formation in 1923. Most of this became the London Midland Region of British Railways, when nationalisation took place in 1948. There was no passenger service between Coventry and Nuneaton from 18th January 1965 to 16th May 1988.

Privatisation resulted in services being provided by Midland Mainline from 2nd April 1996 and by East Midlands Trains from 11th November 2007, between Leicester and Kettering. From Coventry to Leicester, they were worked by Central Trains from 2nd March 1997 until 10th November 2007 Thereafter, Coventry to Nuneaton was worked by London Midland, and Birmingham - Nuneaton - Leicester by CrossCountry Trains.

PASSENGER SERVICES

The tables below give sample figures for trains running on at least five days per week.

Coventry to Nuneaton via Bedworth

	Weekdays	Sundays
1869	9	2
1905	10	2
1935	15	2
1960	25	8
2008	15	8

After trains returned in 1988, three were on offer on weekdays. They soon became hourly, daily.

Nuneaton to Leicester via Hinckley

	Weekdays		Sundays	
	Fast	Slow	Fast	Slow
1876	0	4	0	3
1909	2	11	1	3
1930	3	5	1	4
1960	4	19	3	8
2008	15	16	9	10

Leicester to Rugby via Broughton

	Weekdays	Sundays
1845	8	4
1876	5	2
1905	5	2
1930	7	2
1960	7	0

From 1840 to 1852, the route carried all London-York services, but they ran via Grantham after the East Coast Main Line opened.

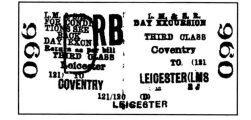

DECEMBER 1, 1841.

No. of Trains.	1	2	3	4	5	6	SUNDAYS. 1	2	3
DOWN TRAINS.	1,2,3 class	1 & 2 class	1 & 2 class	1,2,3 class	1 & 2 class	1 & 2 class	1,2,3 class	1 & 2 class	1 & 2 class
DEPART FROM	am	am	am	am	pm	Mail pm	am	am	Mail pm
London	..	6 0	9 15	11 0	5 0	9 0	..	8 0	9 0
Birmingham	..	8 30	..	1 15	6 0	..	..	..	..
Coventry	..	9 12	..	2 4	6 45	..	..	..	..
Rugby	6 45	9 45	12 50	2 55	8 45	12 20	7 30	12 15	12 20
Ullesthorpe	7 5	10 0	1 10	3 15	9 10	12 40	7 50	12 35	12 40
Broughton	7 15	10 8	..	3 23	..	..	8 0	..	..
Wigston	7 25	10 20	..	3 35	..	..	8 12	..	..
Leicester	7 45	10 40	1 45	3 52	9 40	1 10	8 30	1 10	1 10
Syston	8 0	10 55	2 0	4 5	9 50	1 25	8 45	1 25	1 25
Sileby	8 9	11 4	..	4 15	..	..	8 54	..	..
Barrow	..	11 12	..	4 25	..	..	9 2	..	..
Loughboro'	8 20	11 20	2 18	4 35	10 10	1 45	9 10	1 45	1 45
Kegworth	8 32	11 32	2 30	4 50	10 20	..	9 22	2 0	..
ARRIVE AT									
Nottingham	9 15	12 10	3 15	5 30	10 50	4 10	10 0	2 30	4 10
Derby	9 0	12 10	3 15	5 30	10 50	2 49	10 0	2 30	2 49
Sheffield	11 45	2 45	5 30	8 15	..	5 0	..	5 15	5 0
Leeds	1 30	4 0	7 0	9 45	..	6 19	..	6 45	6 19
York	2 15	4 45	7 45	..	..	6 40	..	7 30	6 40
Darlington	5 45	7 0	..	..	..	9 25	..	..	9 20
Hull	4 15	..	10 5	..	..	8 36	..	10 5	8 36
Manchester	5 0	6 20	8 45	..	..	8 40	..	9 30	..

No. of Trains.	1	2	3	4	5	6	SUNDAYS. 1	2	3
UP TRAINS.	1,2,3 class	1 & 2 class	1,2,3 class	1 & 2 class	1,2,3 class	1 & 2 class	1,2,3 class	1 & 2 class	1 & 2 class
DEPART FROM	am	am	am	am	pm	Mail pm	am	am	Mail pm
Manchester	..	..	7 0	10 30	..	4 45	..	..	..
Hull	..	..	6 0	10 45	..	5 0	..	..	5 0
Darlington	..	..	6 15	9 15	..	3 30	..	..	3 30
York	..	..	8 45	12 0	..	6 19	..	6 45	6 19
Leeds	..	6 0	9 30	1 0	..	7 9	..	7 30	7 9
Sheffield	..	7 30	10 45	1 50	..	8 12	..	8 45	8 12
Derby	8 15	10 45	1 15	4 40	7 30	10 40	6 45	12 15	10 40
Nottingham	8 15	10 40	1 15	4 40	7 30	9 0	6 45	12 15	9 0
Kegworth	8 50	11 18	1 48	5 13	8 5	..	7 25	12 45	..
Loughboro'	9 2	11 30	2 0	5 25	8 17	11 20	7 39	1 0	11 20
Barrow	9 13	..	..	..	8 28	..	7 49	..	..
Sileby	9 20	..	..	..	8 35	..	7 55	..	..
Syston	9 30	11 50	2 20	5 45	8 45	11 45	8 5	1 20	11 45
Leicester	9 50	12 5	2 40	6 0	9 0	12 0	8 30	1 40	12 0
Wigston	10 0	..	..	..	9 10	..	8 40	..	..
Broughton	10 15	..	..	..	9 25	..	8 58	..	..
Ullesthorpe	10 30	12 30	3 15	6 30	9 40	12 30	9 10	2 10	12 30
ARRIVE AT									
Rugby	11 0	12 50	3 40	7 0	10 0	12 50	9 30	2 30	12 50
Coventry	12 35	1 34	6 26	9 2	12 27	..	..	..	..
Birmingham	1 45	2 30	7 45	10 15	1 30	..	..	..	..
London	3 15	6 0	7 45	11 15	..	5 0	1 30	7 30	5 0

NOTTINGHAM TO DERBY.	1,2,3 class	1 & 2 class	1 & 2 class	1,2,3 class	1 & 2 class	SUNDAYS. 1,2,3 class	1,2,3 class	1 & 2 class
DEPART FROM	am	am	pm	pm	pm	am	pm	pm
Nottingham	7 30	10 40	2 45	6 0	9 0	9 0	7 0	9 0
Beeston	7 39	10 49	2 54	6 9	9 9	9 9	7 9	9 9
Long-Eaton	7 48	10 58	3 3	6 18	..	9 18	7 18	..
Sawley	7 56	11 5	3 11	6 26	9 23	9 26	7 26	9 23
Borrowash	8 5	11 15	3 20	6 35	..	9 35	7 35	..
Spondon	..	11 20	..	6 40	..	9 40	7 40	..
ARRIVE AT								
Derby	8 15	11 25	3 30	6 45	9 40	9 45	7 45	9 40

DERBY TO NOTTINGHAM.	1 & 2 class	1,2,3 class	1 & 2 class	1,2,3 class	1 & 2 class	SUNDAYS. 1 & 2 class	1,2,3 class	1,2,3 class
DEPART FROM	am	am	pm	pm	pm	am	am	pm
Derby	3 30	9 0	1 30	4 50	7 30	3 30	9 15	8 0
Spondon	..	9 5	1 35	4 55	..	..	9 20	8 5
Borrowash	..	9 11	1 41	5 3	7 43	..	9 26	8 11
Sawley	..	9 20	1 50	5 10	7 50	..	9 35	8 20
Long-Eaton	..	9 28	1 58	5 20	8 0	..	9 43	8 28
Beeston	..	9 37	2 7	5 28	8 8	..	9 52	8 37
ARRIVE AT								
Nottingham	4 10	9 45	2 15	5 35	8 15	4 10	10 0	8 45

December 1841

BIRMINGHAM, WHITACRE, NUNEATON, and LEICESTER.—Midland.

Miles from Birmingham	Up.	Week Days.										Sundays.			
	Temple Street Station.	mrn	mrn	mrn	mrn	mrn	mrn	aft	aft	aft	aft	mrn	mrn	mrn	aft
	BRISTOL 200....dep	....	....	....	....	7 45	1015	1 30	1 30	3 20	8 0	....	....	....	7 0
	BATH (Mid.) 200 ,,	....	....	....	....	7 25	9 55	1 10	1 10	3 0	6 35	....	....	....	6 40
	GLOUCESTER 200 ,,	....	....	....	....	9 14	1130	2 51	2 51	4 40	8 58	....	....	7 35	8 23
	CHELTENHAM 200 ,,	....	....	....	....	9 25	1142	3 3	3 3	4 52	9 9	....	....	7 47	8 34
	WORCESTER 200 ,,	....	....	....	....	1014	1224	3 46	3 46	5 40	9 47	....	....	8 52	9 19
	From Shrewsbury, p. 18.	mrn	g	g	g	mrn	aft	aft	aft	aft	aft	mrn	mrn	aft	aft
	Birmingham (NewSt.)dp	....	7 20	7 40	8 25	1115	2 25	5 10	5 45	6 45	1119	....	7 40	5 45	1119
2	Saltley	....	7 25	....	a	1120	2 30	5 15	5 50	6 50	Runs *via* Derby.	....	7 45	5 50	Runs *via* Derby.
5¼	Castle Bromwich	....	7 37	....	a	a	2 42	....	6 1	....		....	....	....	
7¾	Water Orton	....	7 43	....	a	a	2 48	....	6 7	....		....	7 57	6 2	
9¼	Forge Mills	....	7 48	....	a h	a	2 53	....	6 12	....		....	8 2	6 7	
10¼	Whitacre	....	8 5	8 5	a	a i	2 58	....	6 17	....		....	8 7	6 12	
12¼	Shustoke	....	8 11		a	a	3 3	....	6 23	k		....	8 13	6 18	
14¼	Arley and Fillongley	....	8 17		....	a	3 9	....	6 29	....		....	8 19	6 24	
19¼	Stockingford..[133, 137	....	8 26		....	a	....	....	6 38	....		....	8 28	6 33	
20¾	Nuneatn (Mid.) 203, 128,	2 10	8 33		....	1155	3 19	....	6 45	7 25		2 10	8 34	6 39	
25½	Hinckley ....[199	2 31	8 44		a	12 5	3 31	a c	7 34			2 31	8 45	6 50	
40	Leicester 203, 186, 189,	2 55	9 10		9 25	1232	4 0	6 17	8 5		1 56	2 55	9 10	7 15	1 56
93	PETERBORO' 203 arr	....	1120		....	2 50	6 55	....	1025		....	....	1145	9 55	....
197	YARMOUTH 94... ,,	....	5 6		....	7 52	....	....	3 30		....	aft {	9 30	3 30	....
133	189 LONDON (St. Pan.) ,,	....	1150		1150	2 55	6 30	8 40	1140		4 45		9 45	10 5	4 45
134¾	189 ,, (MoorgteSt.) ,,	....	12 7		12 7	3 8	6 42	8 57	....		....		10 0	1034	....

Miles from Leicester															
	Moorgate Street Station,	mrn	mrn	mrn	mrn	aft		aft	aft	aft		mrn	aft	aft	aft
	LONDON 186.....dep	....	9 37	1141	1141	2 56		4 7	5 15	8 49		....	2 26	....	8 42
	186 ,, (St. Pan.) ,,	5 15	10 0	12 0	12 0	3 15		4 30	5 30	9 15		....	2 50	5 15	9 15
	YARMOUTH 95... ,,	....	6 0	....	....	....		9 25	....	....		....	....	....	....
	203 PETERBORO' (G.E.) ,,	....	1025	11 5	11 5	....		3 50	7 45	....		7 30	4 40	....	....
	Campbell Street Station,	mrn	aft	aft	aft	aft		aft	aft	aft		mrn	aft	aft	aft
—	Leicester ....dep	8 20	1235	2 8	2 55	5 20		6 40	10 0	1142		1010	7 45	10 0	1142
14½	Hinckley	8 45	1253	b d	3 17	b e		7 11	1025	Runs *via* Derby.		1032	8 8	1025	Runs *via* Derby.
19¼	Nuneaton (Midland) 203	8 58	1 8	....	3 31	....	7 21	7 40	1038			1042	8 19	1038	
20½	Stockingford	9 3	b	....	3 40	....	....	7 45	....			1047	8 24	....	
25¼	Arley and Fillongley	9 12	b	....	3 49	....	....	7 55	....			1056	8 33	....	
27½	Shustoke	9 18	b	....	3 55	l	....	8 2	....			11 2	8 39	....	
29¾	Whitacre 201	9 23	b	....	4 1	....	....	8 7	....			11 6	8 45	....	
30½	Forge Mills	9 28	b	....	4 6	Sat.	b	8 13	....			1112	8 50	....	
32½	Water Orton	9 33	b	....	4 11	....	b	8 18	....			1118	8 55	....	
34¾	Castle Bromwich ..[201	9 39	b	....	4 17	....	b	8 25	....			....	....	....	
38	Saltley [178, 17, 19, 133,	9 45	b	....	4 24	....	7 45	8 32	....	mrn		1129	9 6	....	mrn
40	Birmingham 198, 129, a	9 55	1 45	3 12	4 40	6 27	7 55	8 45	....	1 55		1140	9 20	....	1 55
65½	WORCESTER 198 arr	1122	3 38	5 35	5 50	....	9 11	3 36	....	8 36		6 2	3 36	....	8 36
87½	CHELTENHAM 199 ,,	1213	4 22	6 18	6 27	....	9 50	4 13	....	4 13		7 2	4 13	....	4 13
94	GLOUCESTER 199 ,,	1234	4 42	6 36	6 48	....	10 8	4 34	....	4 34		7 23	4 34	....	4 34
135	BATH (Mid.) 199 ,,	2 55	6 30	8 25	8 25	....	*f* 10	7 10	....	7 10		9 25	7 10	....	7 10
131	199 BRISTOL (Temple St.)	2 10	6 25	7 45	8 0	....	1115	5 45	....	5 45		9 5	5 45	....	5 45

☞ For other Trains between Birmingham and Whitacre, see pages 198 and 201.

a Stop when required to take up for London. **b** Stop when required to set down from London, on informing the Guard at the preceding *stopping* Station. **c** Stops on Thursdays. **d** Stops on Mondays. **e** Stops on Wednesdays and Saturdays to set down, and when required to take up for Birmingham. *f Via* G. W. route. **g** Calls at Welford Road, Leicester, on Wednesdays and Saturdays. **h** Stops on Saturdays. **i** Stops on the 20th inst. to set down when required. **k** Stops when required to set down from Worcester or Stations west thereof on informing the Guard at Saltley. **l** Stops to set down from Bedford or London on informing the Guard at the preceding *stopping* Station.

June 1876

LEICESTER and RUGBY.—Midland.

Mls from Leicester.		mrn	mrn	mrn	mrn	mrn	mrn	mrn	mrn	mrn	aft	aft	aft	aft				mrn	aft	
			Mondays only.				Except Saturdays.	Saturdays only.	Except Saturdays.	Saturdays only.			Except Saturdays.	Saturdays only.	l Leaves at 3 mrn. on Mondays.		SUNDAYS.			
	LEEDS 488 ......dep.	3k18	3 0	4 l 2	4 l 2	8 30	1020	9 37	9 37	1110	2 24	....	4 0	4 20		....		4 15	5 30	....
	DERBY 489 ...... "	3b18	5 50	5 50	8 5	1048	1210	1220	1220	1 40	3 55	4 12	5 50	7 15		....		8 10	7 10	....
	NOTTINGHAM 489 "	4b35	6 38	6h38	7 15	1025	12 0	1232	1232	1 32	3 53	4 45	6 7	7 5		....		8 10	7 38	....
	London Road,	mrn	mrn	mrn	mrn	mrn	aft	aft	aft	aft	aft	aft	aft	aft				mrn	aft	
—	**Leicester** ....dep.	5 55	7 30	7 45	9 5	1140	1 0	1 45	1 45	3 20	5 0	5 40	7 40	8 13		....		9 10	8 40	....
3¼	Wigston South	6 2	7 38	7 53	9 13	1147	1 7	1 52	1 53	3 28	5 8	5 48	7 49	8 22		....		9 17	8 48	....
5¼	Countesthorpe	....	7 44	....	9 20	1153	1 13	2 0		3 34	5 14	....	7 55	8 28		....		9 23	8 54	....
9	Broughton Astley	....	7 51	....	9 27	12 0	1 20	2 8		3 40	5 20	....	:3	8 35		....		9 30	9 2	....
12¾	Ullesthorpe & Lutterwrth	....	7 59	....	9 35	12 6	1 28	2 14		3 48	5 27	....	8 11	8 43		....		9 36	9 12	....
20	**Rugby 360, 369, 436** ar	....	8 12	....	9 48	1218	1 44	2 27		4 2	5 40	....	8 23	8 54		....		9 50	9 26	....
34¾	381 LEAMINGTON* 436 arr.	....	1014	....	1145	1 20	2 54	4 15		4 30	6 12	....	9 58	1212		....		2 30	3 40	....
86¾	OXFORD 378 ..... "	....	1125	....	1217	3 15	4 27	5 30		8 10	9 50	....	11 0	....		....		1245	....	....
102¼	**London** (Eus.) 369 "	....	9 55	....	1245	2 50	4 0	5 15		6 10	8 10	....	1045	3 50		....		1245	3 50	....

b Except Mondays. *h* Leaves at 5 50 mrn. on Saturdays. *k* Leaves at 2 37 mrn. on Mondays. * Avenue Station.

October 1905

BIRMINGHAM, WHITACRE, NUNEATON, and LEICESTER.

Miles.	Up.	Week Days.																					
		mrn	mrn	mrn	mrn	mrn	mrn k	mrn	mrn S	mrn	mrn	mrn	mrn	mrn	mrn k		aft E	aft S	aft	mrn	mrn J	aft	aft E
	660 BRISTOL (Tem. Mead) dep.	...	...	...	...	...	1 10	1 10	...	...	...	...	...	7 40	9 5	...	...	...	...	1025	1025	...	...
—	**Birmingham** (New St.)..dep.	...	...	...	...	...	7 30	7 38	...	8 30	...	9 35	...	1050	1148	...	...	...	...	1 5	1 52	...	...
2	Saltley	...	...	...	...	...	...	7 45	...	...	...	...	...	1056	...	...	...	...	...	1 12	...	...	...
5¼	Castle Bromwich	...	...	...	...	...	7 41	7 51	...	8 40	...	...	...	11 2	...	...	...	...	...	1 18	2 3	...	...
7¾	Water Orton	...	...	...	...	...	...	7 57	...	...	...	...	...	11 7	...	...	...	...	...	1 24	...	...	...
9	Coleshill	...	...	...	...	...	...	8 2	...	...	...	...	...	1111	...	...	...	...	...	1 29	...	...	...
10½	Whitacre	...	...	...	...	...	...	8 6	...	...	...	...	...	1116	...	...	...	...	...	1 35	...	...	...
12	Shustoke	...	...	...	...	...	...	8 12	...	...	...	...	...	1122	...	...	...	...	...	1 41	...	...	...
14½	Arley and Fillongley	...	...	...	...	...	...	8 18	...	...	...	...	...	1128	...	...	...	...	...	1 47	...	...	...
18¾	Stockingford	...	...	...	...	7 28	8 4	8 31	...	9 4	...	...	...	1140	...	...	...	...	...	1 58	...	...	...
—	**Nuneaton** (Trent Val.) dep.	3 0	6 0	642	724	...	...	...	846	...	9 20	...	11 15	...	...	...	1252	1252	1 15	...	...	3 7	4 30
20	Nuneaton **D 412, 423,** 687	...	...	...	...	7 33	8 10	8 36	...	9 9	...	10 8	...	1147	1220	...	...	...	...	2 3	2 28	...	...
25	Hinckley	...	6 11	653	735	7 43	8 20	...	856	9 19	9 32	1019	11 24	1158	1232	...	1 2	1 2	1 25	2S20	2 39	317	4 43
28	Elmesthorpe **C**	...	6 18	7 0	745	...	...	...	9 3	...	9 40	...	11 31	...	...	...	...	1 10	1 34	...	...	325	...
31	Croft	...	6 24	7 8	754	...	8 29	...	9 9	...	9 47	...	11 37	...	...	...	...	1 17	1 42	...	...	331	...
32¾	Narborough	...	6 29	712	8 1	...	8 34	...	914	...	9 53	...	11 42	...	...	...	...	1 23	1 48	...	...	336	...
34¼	Blaby	...	6 33	716	8 7	...	...	...	919	...	9 58	...	11 46	...	...	...	...	1 28	1 53	...	...	341	...
36	Wigston **H**..[**649**, 690, 895	...	6 36	721	812	...	...	...	923	...	10 2	...	11S50	1212	...	...	...	1 32	1 57	...	...	345	...
39½	**Leicester** (L. R.) **642,** arr.	330	6 46	730	824	...	8 46	...	933	9 39	1010	1041	11L56	1220	1251	...	1 23	1 44	2 8	2S51	3 0	354	5 8
137¼	**649 London** (St. Pancras) arr.	725	...	956	...	...	11F2	...	...	1210	1210	1T25	2 10	3 23	3 56	...			4 20	...	...	615	...

Up.	Week Days—*Continued*															Sundays.						
	aft S	aft	aft E	Thro' Exp., Bristol to Leicester, Nottingham, and Lincoln, see pages 662, 645, and 700.	aft W	aft		aft	aft	aft	aft	aft k	aft	aft S	aft V	aft	mrn k	mrn	mrn	aft	aft k	aft	aft
660 BRISTOL (Tem. Mead) dep.	...	1255	...		2 45	...	...	2 45	...	...	...	4 25	...	...	7 20	7E20	1 10	...	8 50	...	2 0	...	7 20
Birmingham (New St.)..dep.	...	3 30	...		4 55	...	...	5 15	...	6 0	...	7 18	...	...	1040	1055	7 2	...	1220	...	5 45	...	1055
Saltley	...	3 37	...		Restaurant Car Bristol to Lincoln.	...	...	...	...	6 9	...	7 25	...	...	1046	...	7 8	...	...	...	5 54	...	...
Castle Bromwich	...	3 43	...			...	...	...	...	6 18	...	...	...	...	...	...	...	...	...	...	...	...	...
Water Orton	...	3 49	...			...	...	5 29	...	6 24	...	7 35	...	...	1055	...	7 17	...	...	...	6 3	...	...
Coleshill	...	3 54	...			...	...	5 34	...	6 29	...	7 40	...	...	...	...	7 22	...	...	...	6 8	...	...
Whitacre	...	4A8	...			...	...	5 39	...	6 34	...	7 45	...	...	11 2	...	7 28	...	...	...	6 13	...	...
Shustoke	...	4 13	...			...	...	5 45	...	6 40	...	7 50	...	...	...		...	...		...	...	...	...
Arley and Fillongley	...	4 19	...			...	...	5 51	...	6 46	...	7 56	...	...	S1110		7 37	...		...	6 25	...	
Stockingford	...	4 31	...			...	...	6 2	...	6 57	...	8 9	...	...	1122	Via Derby.	7 50	...	Via Derby.	...	6 40	...	Via Derby.
Nuneaton (Trent Val.) dep.	4 30	...	...			5 35	...	...	630	...	730	...	912	11 0	...		...	10 9		3 0	...	7 30	
Nuneaton **D 412, 423,** 687	...	4 36	445			...	...	6 8	...	7 1	...	8 15	...	...	1130		7 59	...		...	6 46	...	
Hinckley	4 43	...	456			5 44	...	6 22	642	...	742	8 30	921	1110	1140		8 11	1018		3 10	6 59	7 40	
Elmesthorpe **C**	4 54	...	5 3			5 51	...	...	651	...	750	...	928	...	...	...	8 19	1025	...	3 17	...	7 47	...
Croft	5 0	...	5 9			5 57	...	6 32	659	...	756	...	934	...	...	...	8 26	1031	...	3 23	...	7 53	...
Narborough	5 5	...	514			6 2	...	...	7 5	...	8 1	...	939	...	...	...	8 31	1036	...	3 29	...	7 58	...
Blaby	5 10	...	519			6 6	...	...	710	...	8 6	...	944	...	...	...	...	...	...	...	...	...	...
Wigston **H**..[**649**, 690, 895	5 13	...	524			6 10	...	...	713	...	812	...	948	...	...	...	...	...	...	3 35	...	8 4	...
Leicester (L. R.) **642,** arr.	5 26	...	534		5 55	6 17	...	6 48	722	...	823	8 56	957	...	12Z3	1 40	8 44	1048	2 42	3 44	7 22	8 13	2 0
649 London (St. Pancras) arr.	...	...	...		8X35	8X35	...	9 15	915	...	...	...	...	...	...	4 23	1145	2 32	5 2	8 30	9 52	...	4 55

A Arr. at 3 59 aft. **C** Station for Barwell (2½ miles) and Earl Shilton (1¾ miles). **D** Abbey Street.
E or E Except Sats. F Arr. at 11 35 mrn. on Sats. **H** Glen Parva.
J Through Carriages, Gloucester to Yarmouth, Lowestoft, Norwich, and Cromer, see pages 661, 690, and 1030.
k Through Trains, Birmingham to Peterborough, see page 690. L Arrives at 11 59 mrn. on Saturdays.
S or S Saturdays only. T Arr. at 1 50 aft. on Sats. **V** Thursdays and Saturdays.
W Through Carriage, Bournemouth to Lincoln, see pages 662, 645, and 700. X Arrives at 9 5 aft. on Sats.
Z Sunday mrn. only.

November 1930

September 1956

Table 73 LEAMINGTON SPA, COVENTRY and NUNEATON

Miles		Week Days																							
		TC from Birmingham dep 2 50 am (Table 75) a.m	a.m	TC from Tamworth dep 6 15 am (Table 50) a.m ②		E a.m ②	S a.m ②	E a.m		E a.m ②	E a.m ②	TC from Birmingham dep 7 34 am (Table 75) a.m	a.m a		a.m	a.m	a.m ②		E p.m ②	S p.m TC to Weedon arr 1 50 pm (Table 70)		S p.m P	S p.m ②	p.m a		TC from Tamworth dep 1 35 pm (Table 50) S p.m
	Nuneaton (Trent Val) dep	–	5 25	6 43	..	6 55	7 13	7 15	..	7 27	7 45	–	8 15	..	9 8	..	11 10	..	..		..	12 4	..	1 20	..	2 1
1½	Chilvers Coton	..	5 30	6 47	..	6 59	7 18	7 21	..	7 32	7 50	..	8 20	..	9 6	..	11 13	..	..		..	12 7	..	1 23	..	2 4
3¾	Bedworth	..	5 37	6 52	..	7 6	7 24	7 27	..	7 39	7 58	..	8 25	..	9 11	..	11 18	..	..		..	1212	..	1 28	..	2 9
5	Hawkesbury Lane	..	..	6 56	..	–	7 28	..	..	7 43	8 2	..	..	..	9 15	..	11 22	..	..		..	1210	..	1 32	..	2 13
7½	Foleshill	..	5 47	7 2	..	7 15	7 34	7 38	..	7 51	8 10	..	8 32	..	9 20	..	11 27	..	..		..	1221	..	1 37	..	2 18
8½	Daimler Halt	..	5 51	7 7	..	7 19	7 38	7 43	..	7 55	8 15	..	8 36	..	..	..	..	..	..		..	..	..	..	..	..
9	Coundon Road	–	5 55	7 10	..	7 23	7 41	7 46	..	8 1	8 18	..	8 39	..	9 25	..	11 32	..	..		..	1226	..	1 41	..	2 22
10½	**Coventry** .... arr	..	6 0	7k15	..	7 28	7 46	..	..	8 6	..	..	8 44	..	9 30	..	11c37	..	..		..	1231	..	1 46	..	2 27
	Coventry .... dep	3 22	6 15	..	..	..	..	..	..	..	..	8 32	..	..	..	10 15	..	..	1215	1223	..	..	1 26	2 7	..	..
15½	Kenilworth	..	6 28	..	..	..	..	..	..	..	..	8 44	..	..	..	10A32	..	..	1227	1235	..	..	1 38	2 19	..	..
19	**Leamington Spa C**	..	6 37	..	..	..	..	..	..	..	..	8 52	..	..	..	10 40	..	..	1235	1249	..	..	1 46	2 27	..	..
19¾	**Leamington Spa Av** arr	3 41	6 40	..	..	..	..	..	..	..	..	8 55	..	..	..	10 43	..	..	1238	1252	..	..	1 49	2 30	..	..

	Week Days—*continued*															Sundays										
	S p.m	TC to Napton & Stockton arr 4 41 pm (Table 70) p.m		E p.m ②		E p.m U	p.m	E p.m	TC to Rugby (Mid.) arr 8 10 pm (Table 72) p.m	p.m	p.m		p.m	S p.m	p.m		a.m		p.m	TC from Birmingham dep 2 50 pm (Table 75) p.m	p.m		p.m	p.m	p.m	p.m	
Nuneaton (Trent Val) dep	..	3 12	..	..	..	..	5 10	5 48	..	6 55	–	..	7 55	..	10 8	..	7 10	..	1 44	..	5 22	..	..	..	7 38	9 54	..
Chilvers Coton	..	3 15	..	..	..	..	5 14	5 53	..	6 59	..	..	7 59	..	1013	..	7 14	..	..	..	..	..	..	..	..	..	..
Bedworth	..	3 20	..	..	..	..	5 20	6 0	..	7 5	..	..	8 4	..	1019	..	..	..	..	..	..	..	..	..	..	..	..
Hawkesbury Lane	–	3 24	..	–	..	..	5 25	..	..	7 10	..	..	..	..	..	..	..	..	..	..	..	..	..	..	..	..	..
Foleshill	–	3 30	..	..	..	..	5 32	6A13	..	7 17	..	..	8 11	..	1027	..	7 29	..	1 56	..	5 34	..	..	..	7 50	10 6	..
Daimler Halt	..	..	..	..	..	..	5 36	6 17	..	7 21	..	..	..	..	..	..	..	..	..	..	..	..	..	..	..	..	..
Coundon Road	–	3 35	..	..	..	..	5 39	6 21	..	7 24	..	..	8 16	..	1034	..	7 34	..	2 1	..	5 38	..	..	..	7 56	1012	..
Coventry .... arr	–	3 40	..	..	..	..	5 44	6 26	..	7 29	..	..	8 21	..	1039	..	7 42	..	2 6	..	5 42	..	..	..	8 1	1017	..
Coventry .... dep	2 45	3 47	..	4 33	..	..	5 46	6 30	7 12	7 35	7 58	..	8 35	9 38	1044	..	..	..	2 14	3 33	5 45	..	6 25	7 5	8 5	1024	..
Kenilworth	2 57	3 59	..	4 45	..	5 47	6 0	6 42	7 24	7 47	8 8	..	8 48	9 50	1056	..	..	..	2 26	3 43	5 55	..	6 37	7 15	8 17	1036	..
Leamington Spa C	3 5	4 7	..	4 53	..	5 55	6 9	6 50	7 32	7 55	8 14	..	8 57	9 59	11 4	..	..	..	2 34	3 49	6 1	..	6 45	7 21	8 25	1044	..
Leamington Spa Av arr	3 8	4 10	..	4 56	..	5 58	6 12	6 53	7 35	7 58	8 17	..	9 0	10 2	11 8	..	..	..	2 37	3 52	6 4	..	6 48	7 24	8 28	1047	..

A Fridays only
k Arr 5 minutes *earlier*
a Second class only on Saturdays
C Leamington Spa (Milverton) for Warwick
c 2 minutes later on Saturdays
D Through Carriages to Stoke arr 7 58 pm (Table 50)
E or E Except Saturdays
F Through Carriages to Birmingham arr 8 30 am (Table 75)
F Arr 4 minutes *earlier*
G Through Carriages to Tamworth (L.L.) arr. 1 14 pm (Table 50).
K Through Carriages to Birmingham arr 9 46 am (Table 75)
P Through Carriages to Northampton (Castle) arr 1 36 pm (Table 50)
S or S Saturdays only
T Through Carriages to Manchester (Lon. Rd.) arr 10 20 pm (Table 50)
TC Through Carriages
U Through Carriages from Birmingham dep 5 8 pm (Table 75)
X Through Carriages to Stafford on Fridays and Saturdays (Table 50)
Y Second class only except on Saturdays
Z Through Carriages to Birmingham arr. 8 50 am (Table 75)
② Second class only

1. Coventry to Leicester

COVENTRY

II.   The Avoiding Line shown on map I is seen on this 1946 extract at 1¼ ins to 1 mile. It is marked as a vertical single line track in the eastern part of the city. The northern ¾ of it eventually carried the dual carriageway of the A444. Top right is the West Coast Main Line. Three colliery branches can be found. At the top, near Market End, is Newdigate Colliery, where coal was raised from 1901 to 27th June 1981. The branch then closed and coal was moved underground to Coventry Colliery, west of Exhall. This had been the Warwickshire Coal Company. Wyken Colliery was near Hawkesbury. The line ending near the right border received coal from Craven Colliery until 1928 and Alexandra Colliery until 1914, with narrow gauge lines. The latter were rope hauled, to a large extent.

1. There were electric trams operating from 1895 until 1940. Nazi bombing was severe thereon and a high proportion of the buildings in the district were destroyed. However, the station survived, unlike the cathedral. This is the north elevation in about 1900. (P.Laming coll.)

2. A train runs in from the west. Flat wagons were once provided for the horse-drawn coaches of the wealthy gentry. The two through lines were lost during the reconstruction in the early 1960s. (P.Laming coll.)

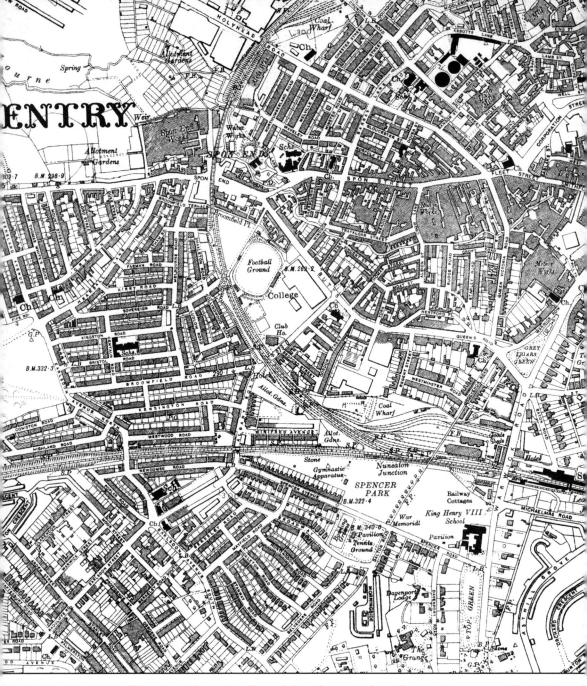

III. The 1938 edition is at 6ins to 1 mile and thus does not show the street tramways. The 1832 route of the L&BR is across both pages. The 1850 line to Nuneaton curves across the top of the left page. Many motor works can be found. The engine shed is to the right of the join in the maps. It was completed by the LNWR in 1897 and coded 2D when closed on 17th November 1958. The small MR shed was east of Warwick Road. The Avoiding Line is almost parallel to the right border.

➔ IV. The B4109 is top right on map II and on the right of this 1936 extract at 20ins to 1 mile. It shows the details of the Avoiding Line's northern depot, marked on map I. It closed on 5th July 1965. The southern one is on the map above, near its right border. The siding on the right was used by the city's ballast tram. Trams ran north to Bedworth, running almost to the south end of the High Street.

Bell Green
Goods Station

3.   The LNWR and the MR ran a joint service between Leamington Spa and Nuneaton; it was still in operation when photographed on 4th October 1958. The driver used the compartment on the right. (H.F.Wheeller/R.S.Carpenter)

Other views of Coventry can be seen in our *Rugby to Birmingham* album.

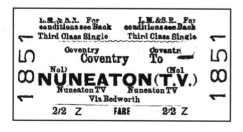

4.   A class 5 4-6-0 runs in from Nuneaton with an excursion returning from Blackpool on 3rd September 1960. No. 3 Box had 38 levers and closed on 4th September 1961. A temporary box took over until 15th April 1962, when a new panel box opened. It was on the site of the LNWR engine shed. The West Midlands Signalling Centre at Saltley took over the area on 29th August 2007. Five sidings were still in place in 2013. (H.F.Wheeller/R.S.Carpenter)

5.   The eastward view from platform 4 on 28th September 1994 includes the architectural detail which is tidy and unfussy; even the liftshafts are unobtrusive. Sprinter DMU no. 150102 occupies platform 2 with the 12.16 to Lincoln, which will follow the route of this volume to Leicester. The Regional Railways service from Lincoln was cut back to terminate at Leicester on privatisation. (A.C.Hartless)

6.   On the same day, no. 321420 is seen approaching platform 1 with the 12.36 Birmingham to Euston, illustrating the trackwork at the west end of the station. The train is crossing the junction with the Nuneaton line. The land to the right was previously occupied by the goods yard, and the long footbridge crossed this as well as the running lines. The yard had been fenced off by the time of this picture and subsequently became a retail park. Electric services began in 1966. (A.C.Hartless)

7.   Coventry station was completely rebuilt following World War II damage and was finished in 1962, ahead of electrification of the old London & Birmingham Railway. As constructed, the station formed the south side of Station Square, with office blocks on the square's north side, overlooking the city's formidable inner ring road on their far side. By June 2016, these offices had been demolished, leaving space to appreciate the station's monolithic north elevation. A new foyer was completed in 2016. (A.C.Hartless)

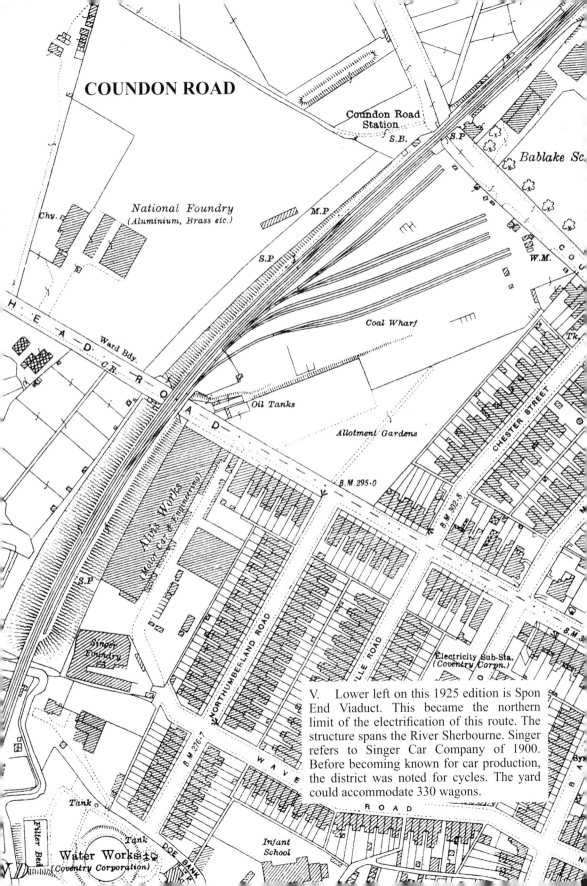

COUNDON ROAD

Coundon Road
Station

S.B.

S.P

Bablake Sc.

National Foundry
(Aluminium, Brass etc.)

Chy.

M.P.

S.P.

W.M.

COU

H

E

A

D

C.R.

Ward Bdy.

R

O

A

D

Coal Wharf

Tk.

Oil Tanks

Allotment Gardens

Chester Street

B.M. 295.0

B.M. 302.8

Alvis Works
(Motor Car & Engineering)

S.P.

Northumberland Road

LLE ROAD

Electricity Sub-Sta.
(Coventry Corpn.)

Singer
Foundry

B.M. 276.7

B.M. 3

By

BA

WAVE

ROAD

Tank

Filter Bed

Tank

DOE BANK

Infant
School

Water Works
(Coventry Corporation)

V.   Lower left on this 1925 edition is Spon
End Viaduct. This became the northern
limit of the electrification of this route. The
structure spans the River Sherbourne. Singer
refers to Singer Car Company of 1900.
Before becoming known for car production,
the district was noted for cycles. The yard
could accommodate 330 wagons.

8.   A view south from 1st November 1958 includes the 1876 signal box, which had 23 levers and was in use until 26th May 2009. It was demolished on 26th January 2014. The spelling was Coun**den** until 1894. (H.F.Wheeller/R.S.Carpenter)

9.   In January 1857, the station became the temporary terminus on the route, when the nearby Spon End Viaduct collapsed. The station was rebuilt in 1896 after the original buildings were destroyed by fire. Closure to passengers came on 18th January 1965. The photo is from 1959. (R.S.Carpenter)

10. A Coventry Corporation bus waits at the level crossing on 26th August 1961, being too tall for the bypass bridge. The coal yard remained open until 30th November 1964. (P.Kingston)

VI. This 1910 plan relates to the 1861 siding to Widdington Cotton Mill. It later became a Daimler factory.

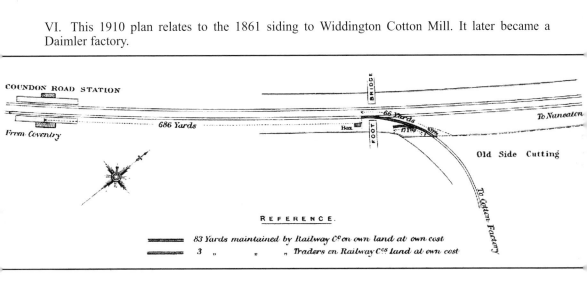

COUNDON ROAD STATION

From Coventry

686 Yards

BRIDGE

FOOT

Hox.

66 Yards

To Nuneaton

Old Side Cutting

To Cotton Factory

REFERENCE.

— 83 Yards maintained by Railway Co on own land at own cost

— 3 „ „ „ Traders on Railway Co's land at own cost

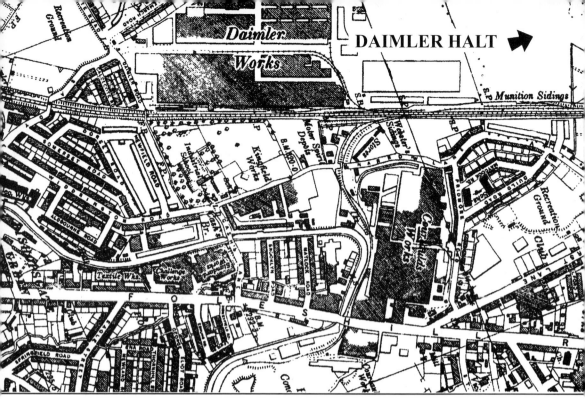

VII. The halt came into use for workers only, on 19th March 1917, and access was by steps to each platform from Sandy Lane, seen top left. The public were allowed to use the services here from 11th June 1956. On Mondays to Fridays, 12 down trains stopped here, between 6.19am and 7.17pm. This 1940 edition is at 8ins to 1 mile.

11. A view north on 7th July 1954 includes one of the two ticket offices, which were entirely white. Closure came on 18th January 1965. The Daimler company was formed in 1896 to build commercial vehicles and luxurious cars. It became part of BSA in 1910, but the name was kept in use. After World War I, it returned to limousine production and continued under the name of Jaguar from 1960. Such cars were built here until July 2005. The Daimler siding was north of the halt, on the west side of the main line. The siding at the bottom of the map served Heath Concrete Works, Webster's Brick Works, an Ordnance Works at Priestley's Bridge and Courtaulds. The latter had two Pecketts until about 1970. (P.Glenn/R.S.Carpenter)

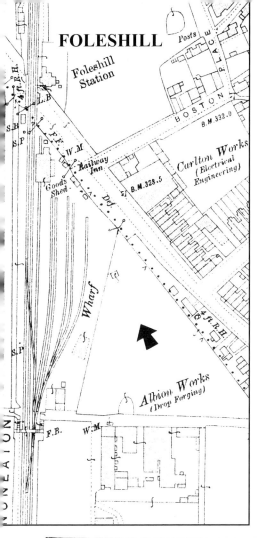

FOLESHILL

12. A panorama from the 1950s includes the loading gauge and still much demand for coal, although it had to be unloaded by shovel. The yard closed on 6th January 1965 and the station followed two weeks later. In the background is the Railway Inn. Two 10-ton cranes were listed in 1938. (A.Dudman coll.)

VIII. The 1913 survey shows a shelter only on the down platform and no footbridge to the up one. It came in 1931, with the road bridge over the line. "Wharf" refers to the coal yard and W.M. to the weighing machine for carts and lorries. The 45-lever signal box shown closed on 26th April 1966.

13. Working a Nuneaton to Coventry train on 10th November 1958 is class 2 2-6-2T no. 41226. The fire buckets are hanging on the GENTS, while washing hangs in the gardens; it must be a Monday.
(H.F.Wheeller/R.S.Carpenter)

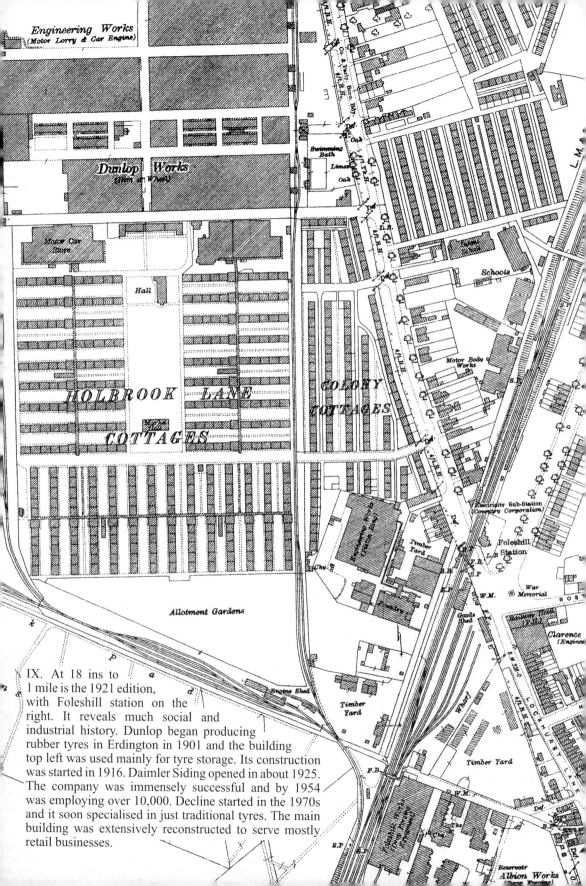

Engineering Works
(Motor Lorry & Car Engines)

Dunlop Works
(Rim or Wharf)

Motor Car Store

Hall

Swimming Bath

Infant School

Schools

Motor Body Works

HOLBROOK   LANE

COTTAGES

COLONY COTTAGES

Electricity Sub-Station
(Coventry Corporation)

Foleshill Station

Timber Yard

War Memorial

Allotment Gardens

Goods Shed

Railway Hotel (P.H.)

Clarence (Engines)

IX. At 18 ins to
1 mile is the 1921 edition,
with Foleshill station on the
right. It reveals much social and
industrial history. Dunlop began producing
rubber tyres in Erdington in 1901 and the building
top left was used mainly for tyre storage. Its construction
was started in 1916. Daimler Siding opened in about 1925.
The company was immensely successful and by 1954
was employing over 10,000. Decline started in the 1970s
and it soon specialised in just traditional tyres. The main
building was extensively reconstructed to serve mostly
retail businesses.

Engine Shed

Timber Yard

Wharf

Timber Yard

Reservoir

Albion Works

14.   Northwest of Foleshill was Coventry Colliery, mentioned in map caption II. It had a 2ft gauge railway serving the surface stockyard. First worked by an Orenstein & Koppel 0-4-0WT purchased secondhand in 1929, it was replaced with a "Resilient" class Fowler four-wheel diesel in 1938. Named *Coventry No. 7*, it is seen here dumped out of use on 1st March 1959 and was sent for scrap soon after. (J.A.Peden/A.Neale)

15.   Coventry Colliery acquired three of the nine class 1501 GWR-designed pannier tanks, after their withdrawal by BR in 1961. Built in 1949, these were the only pannier tanks with outside cylinders. The trio were replaced by diesels in 1970, when nos 1502 and 1509 were scrapped, but no. 1501 was saved by the Severn Valley Railway. (A.Neale coll.)

16.   After Coventry Colliery closed, the site was redeveloped as a distribution park. The rail link from Three Spires Junction was retained and, for several years, trainloads of bottled mineral water ran from France to the site. Class 60 haulage was preferred because of the gradient on the branch. No. 60034 shunts empty vans at the terminus on 29th May 2007, before departing for Wembley Yard. The water traffic ran from February 2007, but ceased in 2009 and the branch became disused. (P.D.Shannon)

Three Spires Junction

17.   We look south on 17th June 1959, with the Coventry Avoiding Line curving to the left. The 1914 box had 53 levers, which were replaced by a panel in 1988. (H.F.Wheeller/R.S.Carpenter)

18. The signalman's coal store becomes more apparent in this view from 24th May 1963. Working the 5.0pm Coventry to Nuneaton Trent Valley is 'Patriot' class 4-6-0 no. 45530 *Sir Frank Ree*. (H.F.Wheeller/R.S.Carpenter)

19.   Seen from the same bridge used for picture 17, but on 16th June 1984, is no. 33027 with the 'Birmingham Boomerang' railtour. The box was destroyed by arsonists on 1st November 1998. A Portakabin was in use from 23rd February 2003 until 28th May 2009. (J.Whitehouse)

20. No. 58022 comes off the Coventry Colliery branch at Three Spires Junction with a Merry-Go-Round coal train for Didcot Power Station on 19th August 1985. The branch had been added to the rail network after World War I and became busy with traffic from the colliery, as well as to and from the adjacent Homefire smokeless fuel plant. In the 1980s, much of the coal from Coventry Colliery went to Didcot, but some went to Garston Docks for export to Northern Ireland. The colliery closed in 1991. Visible just above the third wagon is the diminutive Bedlam Gates box, which closed on 13th November 1988. It had six levers. (P.D.Shannon)

X.   Official RCH siding list for the Coventry and Foleshill areas in 1938.

Building Trades Supply Co. (L. M. S., L. N. W.).........	Foleshill Railway Co.'s Siding.
Cattle Sales Sid. (LMS, LNW)	Coventry and Coundon Road.
Courtauld. S.. & Co.'s Siding (L. M. S., L. N. W.)...	Foleshill Railway Co.'s Siding.
Coventry Co-operative Socy. (L.M.S., L.N.W.)	Foleshill Railway Co.'s Siding.
Coventry Corporation Abattoir	Coventry and Coundon Road.
Daimler Co.'s Siding (L.M.S., L. N. W.).....................	Foleshill and Coundon Road.
Dorrington. W. (LMS,LNW)	Foleshill Railway Co.'s Siding.
Foleshill Railway Co.'s Siding (L. M. S., L. N. W.)	Coventry and Nuneaton.
Gray, J. G. (L.M.S., L.N.W.)	Foleshill Railway Co.'s Siding.
Green, W. H. (L.M.S., LNW)	Foleshill Railway Co.'s Siding.
Hall, G. J. N. (L. M. S., L. N. W.).....................	Foleshill Railway Co.'s Siding.
Hallam & Co. (LMS, LNW)	Foleshill Railway Co.'s Siding.
Heath Concrete Co. (L.M.S., L.N.W.)	Foleshill Railway Co.'s Siding.
Jones, W. H., & Son (L.M.S., L.N.W.)	Foleshill Railway Co.'s Siding.
Jones, Whitby, Ltd. (L.M.S., L. N. W.)	Foleshill Railway Co.'s Siding.
Limmer & Trinidad Lake Asphalt Co., Ltd., Siding (L. M. S., L. N. W.).........	Foleshill Railway Co.'s Siding.
Morton, J., & Son (L. M. S., L. N. W.).....................	Foleshill Railway Co.'s Siding.
Neuchatel Asphalte Co., Ltd. Siding (L. M. S., L. N. W.)	Foleshill Railway Co.'s Siding.

Siding (L. M. S., L. N. W.)	Foleshill Railway Co.'s Siding.
Redline — Glico, Ltd. (L.M.S., L. N. W.).........	Foleshill Railway Co.'s Siding.
Shell-Mex & B. P., Ltd. (L. M. S., L. N. W.)	Foleshill Railway Co.'s Siding.
Stanley Bros. (LMS.LNW)	Foleshill Railway Co.'s Siding.
Ward Bros. (L.M.S., L.N.W.	Foleshill Railway Co.'s Siding
Webster's Brick Works (L.M.S., L.N.W.)	Foleshill Railway Co.'s Siding
Whitley Wharf (LMS,LNW)	Coventry and Brandon.
Wormells, Ltd. (L. M. S., L. N. W.)	Foleshill Railway Co.'s Siding

Foleshill (L. M. S., L. N. W.)	{ L. M. S. (L. N. W.)...... L. M. S. (Mid.)............
Brett's Patent Lifter Co.'s Siding	L. M. S. (L. N. W.).........
Clarke, W., & Son	L. M. S. (L. N. W.).........
Coventry Corporation Gas Works (L.M.S., L.N.W.)..	L. M. S. (L. N. W.–Mid.)
Dunlop Rim & Wheel Co., Ltd.	L. M. S. (L. N. W.) ......
Dunlop Rubber Co.'s Siding	L. M. S. (L. N. W.) ......
Pearsons & Burden	L. M. S. (L. N. W.).........
Warwickshire Coal Co.'s Coventry Coll. (Keresley)	L. M. S. (L. N. W.).........
Whitmore Park Estate Co., Ltd., Siding..................	L. M. S. (L. N. W.) ......
Wormell, W. J. & R.	L. M. S. (L. N. W.).........

21. No. 58010 draws to a halt at Bedlam Gates Crossing, having just set back out of the headshunt at Three Spires Junction on 16th April 1986. The train is the 13.30 from Three Spires Junction to Didcot, carrying coal from Coventry Colliery. The A444 road bridge would later be built on this site. (P.D.Shannon)

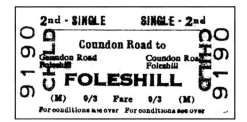

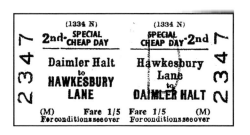

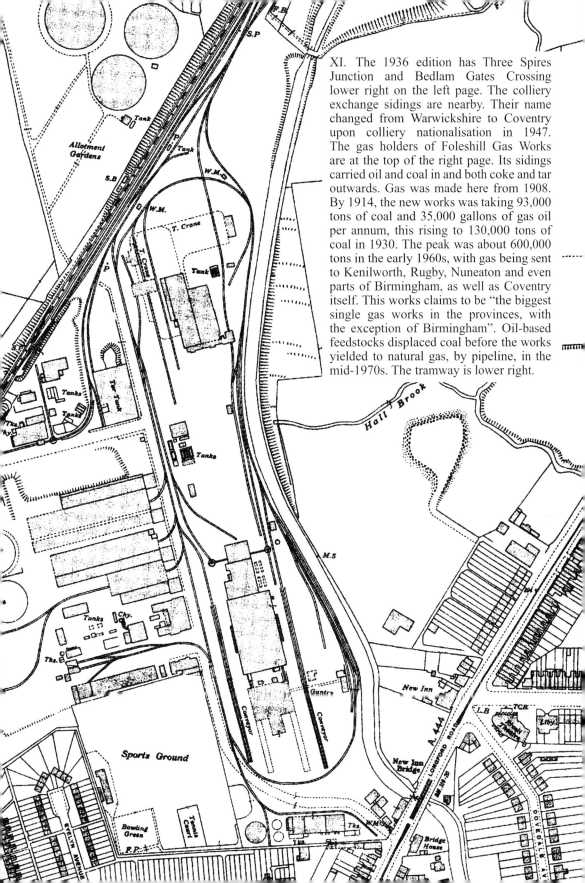

XI. The 1936 edition has Three Spires Junction and Bedlam Gates Crossing lower right on the left page. The colliery exchange sidings are nearby. Their name changed from Warwickshire to Coventry upon colliery nationalisation in 1947. The gas holders of Foleshill Gas Works are at the top of the right page. Its sidings carried oil and coal in and both coke and tar outwards. Gas was made here from 1908. By 1914, the new works was taking 93,000 tons of coal and 35,000 gallons of gas oil per annum, this rising to 130,000 tons of coal in 1930. The peak was about 600,000 tons in the early 1960s, with gas being sent to Kenilworth, Rugby, Nuneaton and even parts of Birmingham, as well as Coventry itself. This works claims to be "the biggest single gas works in the provinces, with the exception of Birmingham". Oil-based feedstocks displaced coal before the works yielded to natural gas, by pipeline, in the mid-1970s. The tramway is lower right.

22. Running north is a class 47 diesel with a Cross Country express. 'All Change' is apparent, including a bridge under construction in the background. No. 47823 is working the 06.40 Poole to Manchester on 27th January 1990. (J.Whitehouse)

Coventry Avoiding Line

23. This route is mentioned in map caption I and it very seldom carried passenger trains. Southbound on 2nd June 1957 is 'The Mercian', an RCTS Railtour hauled by class 5 4-6-0 no. 45091. Part of the Bell Green Depot is on the left and is on map IV. (H.F.Wheeller/R.S.Carpenter)

COVENTRY ARENA

24. London Midland single car no. 153365 passes the site of Three Spires Junction running to Coventry on 12th August 2015. On the left, the overgrown track of the former Coventry Colliery branch can just be made out. (P.D.Shannon)

25. Coventry Arena station opened on 18th January 2016. It serves the adjacent Ricoh Arena (the stadium for Coventry City Football Club and Wasps Rugby Union FC) and also a retail park on the opposite side of the tracks. The platforms have identical modular shelters and are linked by a path beneath a pre-existing occupation bridge to their south. London Midland's stock disposition has limited the service provision to a single car working an hourly shuttle, which is of little use for match days. Here, no. 153365 arrives with 11.14 Nuneaton-Coventry, on 6th June 2016. (A.C.Hartless)

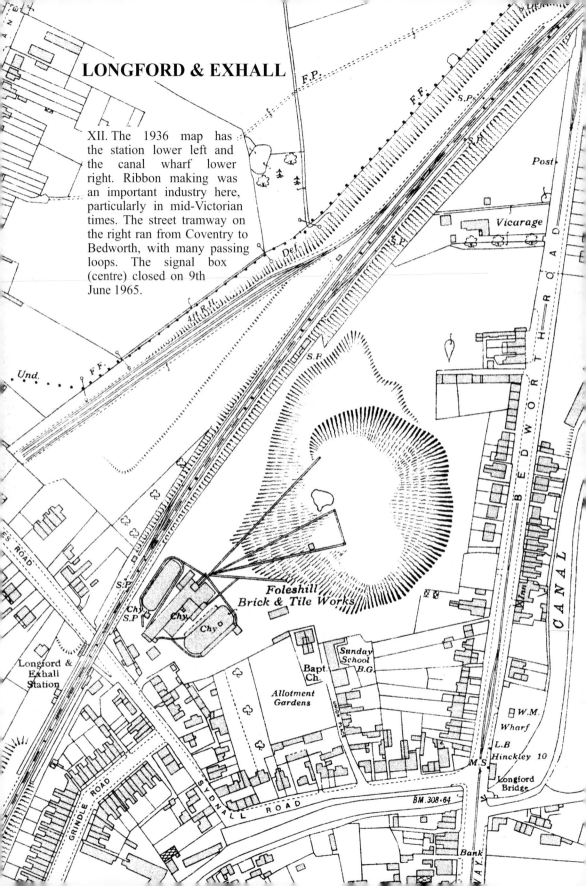

LONGFORD & EXHALL

XII. The 1936 map has the station lower left and the canal wharf lower right. Ribbon making was an important industry here, particularly in mid-Victorian times. The street tramway on the right ran from Coventry to Bedworth, with many passing loops. The signal box (centre) closed on 9th June 1965.

Foleshill
Brick & Tile Works

Longford &
Exhall
Station

Sunday
School
B.G

Bapt.
Ch.

Allotment
Gardens

Vicarage

Post

BEDWORTH ROAD

CANAL

W.M.
Wharf

L.B
Hinckley 10
M.S

Longford
Bridge

BM.308·64

Bank

GRINDLE ROAD

SYDNALL ROAD

26.   This southward panorama from 1950 has a Foleshill gas holder in the background and the road underbridge in the foreground. There was an approach road to the buildings on the left and steps to the platform on the right. Trains ceased to call on 23rd May 1949. (R.M.Casserley coll.)

LEAMINGTON SPA, COVENTRY, and NUNEATON

Down

	Week Days		Sundays	
Leamington Spa......dep.	(various times)			A 1¼ miles to Coventry Road Sta
Warwick (Milverton) A				B Trent Valley; about 1¼ miles to Abbey Street Sta
Kenilworth				D Thurs. and Sats.
Coventry 474, 475 {arr. / dep				E or E Except Sats
Coundon Road				S or S Sats only
Foleshill				U 6 mins later on Sats.
Longford and Exhall				X 10 mins earlier Sats.
Hawkesbury Lane				Y 5 mins later on Sats.
Bedworth				Z 10 mins later on Sats
Chilvers Coton (689				
Nuneaton				

Up

Miles		Week Days		Sundays	
	Nuneaton (Trent Val.)..dep				
1¼	Chilvers Coton				
3¾	Bedworth				
5	Hawkesbury Lane				
5½	Longford and Exhall				
7½	Foleshill				
8½	Coundon Road				
10	Coventry 474, 475 {arr. / dep				
15½	Kenilworth				
18½	Warwick (M.) A 98. [below]				
19½	Leamington Spa 103, arr.				

January 1935

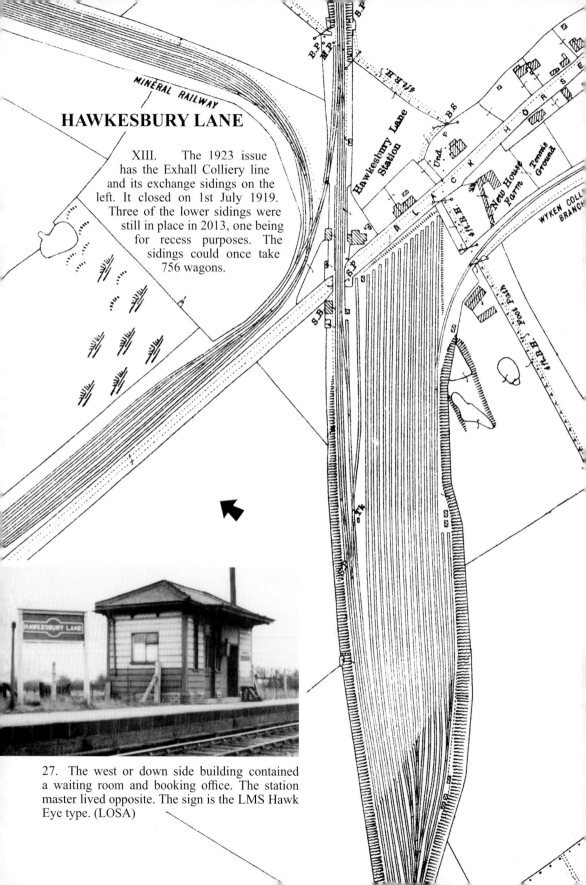

HAWKESBURY LANE

XIII. The 1923 issue has the Exhall Colliery line and its exchange sidings on the left. It closed on 1st July 1919. Three of the lower sidings were still in place in 2013, one being for recess purposes. The sidings could once take 756 wagons.

27. The west or down side building contained a waiting room and booking office. The station master lived opposite. The sign is the LMS Hawk Eye type. (LOSA)

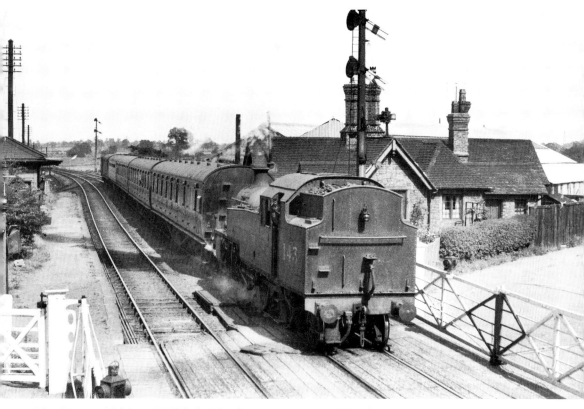

28.   Seen on 24th May 1948 is 2-6-2T class 3P no. 143, working the 2.55pm Nuneaton to Coventry. Passenger trains ceased to call here on 18th January 1965. (SLS coll.)

29.   No. 31160 speeds south with a Newcastle to Poole express on a Saturday in a Summer around 1970. Goods ceased here on 4th January 1965. The 1896 box had a 26-lever frame, which functioned until 26th May 2009. (J.Whitehouse)

SOUTH OF BEDWORTH

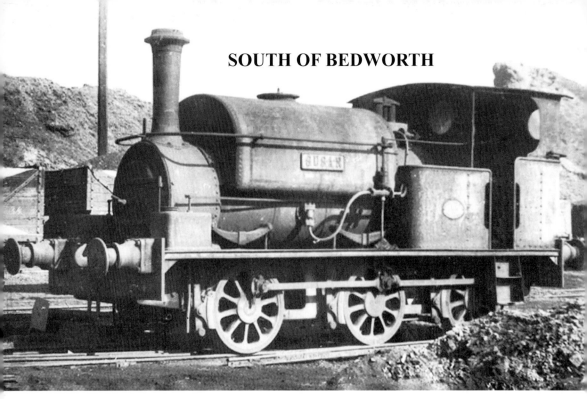

30. Newdigate Colliery was west of the main line and open from 1898 to 1982. This is a picture of Hudswell Clarke 0-6-0ST *Susan*, supplied new in 1902, photographed in 1953 and scrapped in 1958. (A.Neale coll.)

31. DB no. 66112 is seen at the Murco Oil Terminal ready to form the 16.08 empty train to Robeston on 20th April 2016. The location handled Calor Gas. (A.J.Whitehouse)

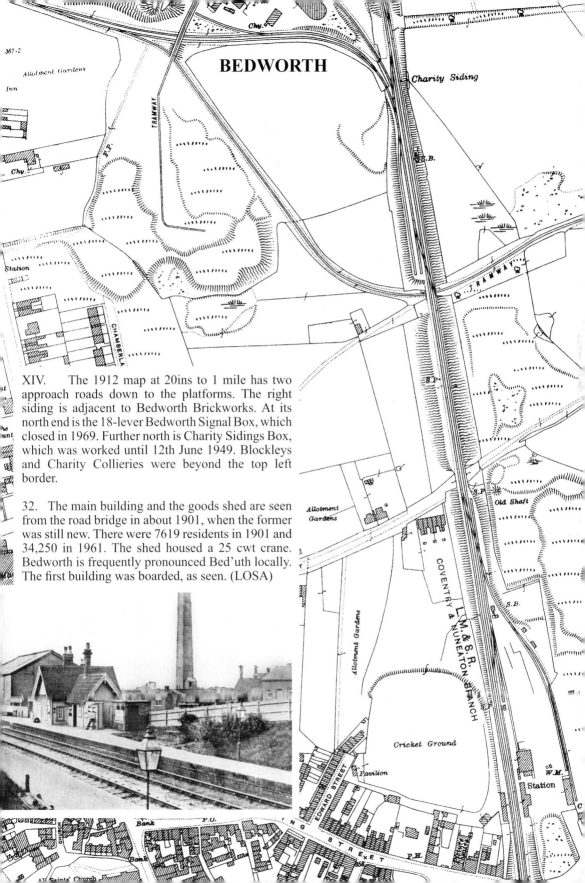

BEDWORTH

Charity Siding

S.B.

TRAMWAY

B.P.

Allotment Gardens

Old Shaft

COVENTRY & NUNEATON BRANCH L. M. & S. R.

S.B.

Allotment Gardens

Cricket Ground

Pavilion

EDWARD STREET

W.M.

Station

XIV.   The 1912 map at 20ins to 1 mile has two approach roads down to the platforms. The right siding is adjacent to Bedworth Brickworks. At its north end is the 18-lever Bedworth Signal Box, which closed in 1969. Further north is Charity Sidings Box, which was worked until 12th June 1949. Blockleys and Charity Collieries were beyond the top left border.

32.   The main building and the goods shed are seen from the road bridge in about 1901, when the former was still new. There were 7619 residents in 1901 and 34,250 in 1961. The shed housed a 25 cwt crane. Bedworth is frequently pronounced Bed'uth locally. The first building was boarded, as seen. (LOSA)

33.   Class 2 2-6-2T no. 41320 heads the 3.12pm Nuneaton to Napton & Stockton, via Kenilworth, on 5th September 1957. Passenger service ceased on 18th January 1965; goods had ended two weeks earlier. (H.B.Priestley/R.Humm)

34.   New platforms opened on 16th May 1988. No. 150105 is calling with 07.40 Derby-Coventry, via Leicester, whilst a hybrid first generation power twin DMU departs forming 08.55 Coventry-Stafford, on 16th May 1988. Temporary closure took place on 23rd May 2004. New shelters and seats arrived in 2005 ready for reopening on 13th June. (A.C.Hartless)

BERMUDA PARK

35.   Like Coventry Arena, Bermuda Park opened on 18th January 2016. It is on the site of Griff Junction and, although sounding exotic, it serves an industrial estate and distribution centre. The name derives from former landowner Edward Newdigate, one time Governor of Bermuda, and was given to a nearby pit village in 1893. No. 153366 arrives with 14.42 Coventry to Nuneaton on 20th April 2016. (J.Whitehouse)

36.   Local freight traffic had dwindled away, but longer distance hauls could still be seen. No. 66076 powers through with the 09.15 Manchester Trafford Park to Southampton Western Docks container service on 6th June 2016. (A.C.Hartless)

XVa. The 1946 edition is at 2ins to 1 mile and has our route from lower centre to top right. Lower left is Griff Colliery. Some of its pits were sunk in the era prior to the railway. No. 4 was in use in 1850 and No. 5 in 1870. The LNWR branch opened to the Tile Works (left: known as Stanley's Brick Siding) on 22nd June 1881 and was soon to serve Griff Colliery and the brick works. Colliery locos worked all the lines and the traffic included moving colliery waste to the clay pits. Ten different colliery engines worked the lines, but from the early 1950s, main line locomotives ran between the colliery sidings and the various users. These ranged from power stations to ironstone works. The lower part of the triangular junction, which is seen to pass under the main line, closed on 4th March 1968. The 25-lever Griff Junction Box closed on 3rd February 1985.

37. Hunslet 0-6-0ST *Britannia* of 1879 spent its entire career at Griff Colliery, until scrapped in 1956. Clara Pit was southwest of that, close to Griff. The big No. 4 Pit was one mile southwest of it. (A.Neale coll.)

CHILVERS COTON

38. This footbridge arrived around 1930. The photo was taken soon after closure on 18th January 1965. The position of the door of the gents toilet indicates its closure. (R.Humm coll.)

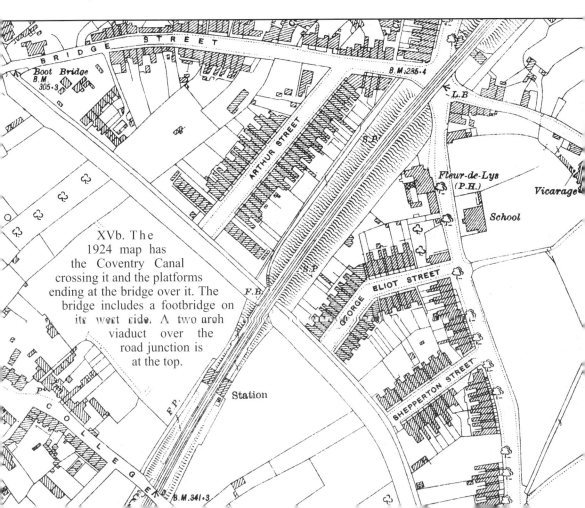

XVb. The 1924 map has the Coventry Canal crossing it and the platforms ending at the bridge over it. The bridge includes a footbridge on its west side. A two arch viaduct over the road junction is at the top.

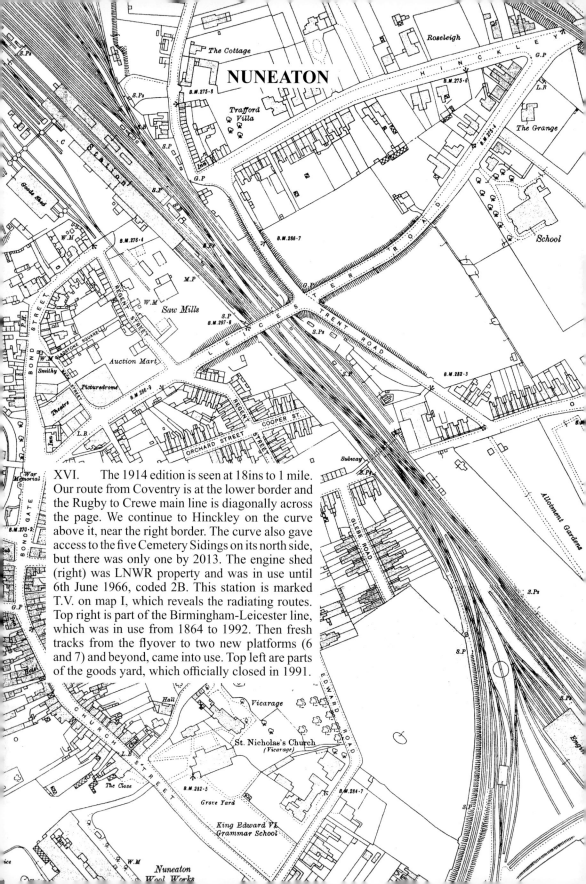

NUNEATON

XVI. The 1914 edition is seen at 18ins to 1 mile.
Our route from Coventry is at the lower border and
the Rugby to Crewe main line is diagonally across
the page. We continue to Hinckley on the curve
above it, near the right border. The curve also gave
access to the five Cemetery Sidings on its north side,
but there was only one by 2013. The engine shed
(right) was LNWR property and was in use until
6th June 1966, coded 2B. This station is marked
T.V. on map I, which reveals the radiating routes.
Top right is part of the Birmingham-Leicester line,
which was in use from 1864 to 1992. Then fresh
tracks from the flyover to two new platforms (6
and 7) and beyond, came into use. Top left are parts
of the goods yard, which officially closed in 1991.

39.   The main line station opened on 15th September 1847 and was subjected to many alterations, particularly regarding platforms. The suffix 'Trent Valley' was in use from 2nd June 1924 until 5th May 1969. (LOSA)

40.   A 1970 panorama southwards records the platform improvements that took place just prior to the electrification of the main line from Rugby. The overhead lines were in use from 16th November 1964. The goods yard closed for public traffic on 2nd October 1972, but ballast was handled until 1991. (Stations UK)

41. The 1915 frontage was photographed on 21st June 1977, by when traffic was starting to increase. The annual usage exceeded one million passengers from 2012-13. Abbey Street station is shown on map I. (H.C.Casserley)

42. We now have two views from 25th February 2014. Waiting at Platform 1 to depart for Coventry is no. 153375. The other clock face was of greater use. Lift space was generous from the outset. Through running between Coventry and Hinckley, by reversal here, ceased when many of the crossovers on the main line were removed during its upgrading in 2003-04. (P.Jones)

43. Standing at the north end of the new platform number 6 is a Bombardier Adtranz class 170 unit. It is working from Leicester to Birmingham. Nos 6 and 7 would take seven coaches, nos 2 to 5 from 12 to 17, but no. 1 was limited to eight. Nos 4 and 5 had been added in 1868 and nos 6 and 7 opened on 7th June 2004. (P.Jones)

Signal Boxes

Nuneaton Power Signal Box had a panel in use from 1963 to 2008, when Rugby Signalling Control Centre took over.

	No. of levers	Closure
No. 1	180	1963
No. 2	40	1961
No. 3	145	1963
Down Sidings	62	1963
Up Sidings	39	1963
Midland Junction	29	1992
Nutts Lane	25	1960

For other views see *Birmingham to Tamworth and Nuneaton* **and** *Rugby to Stafford* **albums.**

182   182

L.M.&S.R. For conditions see Back
PRIVILEGE TICKET
Valid 7 days
Third Class Single

L.M.&S.R. For conditions see Back
PRIVILEGE TICKET
Valid 7 days
Third Class Single

Hawkesbury L.
Hawkesbury Lane   **To**
NUNEATON (T.V.)
Nuneaton TV   Nuneaton TV
·3 7   FARE   ·3 Z

MY.22. 00   035

LONDON & NORTH WESTERN RY
ONE BICYCLE, PERAMBULATOR, OR CHILD'S MAIL CART, ACCOMPANIED BY PASSENGER, AT OWNER'S RISK.
LONGFORD & EXHALL TO
ANY L&NW STATION ABOVE 12 & NOT MORE THAN 25 MILES DISTANT
CARRIAGE PAID -/9
This ticket must be given up on arrival
TURN OVER)

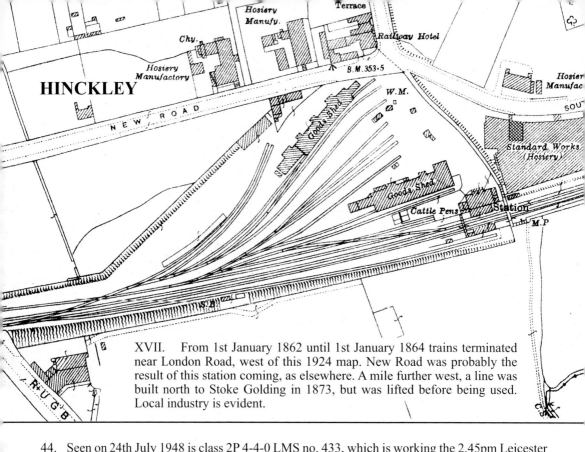

HINCKLEY

XVII.   From 1st January 1862 until 1st January 1864 trains terminated near London Road, west of this 1924 map. New Road was probably the result of this station coming, as elsewhere. A mile further west, a line was built north to Stoke Golding in 1873, but was lifted before being used. Local industry is evident.

44.   Seen on 24th July 1948 is class 2P 4-4-0 LMS no. 433, which is working the 2.45pm Leicester to Nuneaton service. The population was 11,304 in 1901 and 42,000 in 1961. A notable long-distance train called here at 2.39pm on weekdays in 1930. It ran from Gloucester to Lowestoft. (W.A.Camwell/SLS)

45. No. 37172 is hauling domestic coal towards Nuneaton sometime in the 1970s. The footbridge was replaced by one devoid of steps in about 1983. (J.Whitehouse)

46. No. 156417 is working the 09.16 Coventry to Lincoln on 8th February 1992. On the left is the 1894 signal box, which had 20 levers and closed on 31st July 2006. (M.J.Stretton)

47. The station building is seen on 9th July 2009 and is as substantial as it was for its opening in 1864. However, the premises left of the three-storey section and those at far right, beyond the gable marked 'Moore Scott', were added in 1990 for commercial use. Passenger usage had reached 0.3 million by 2014-15 and the ticket office was still open on weekday mornings. (A.C.Hartless)

ELMESTHORPE

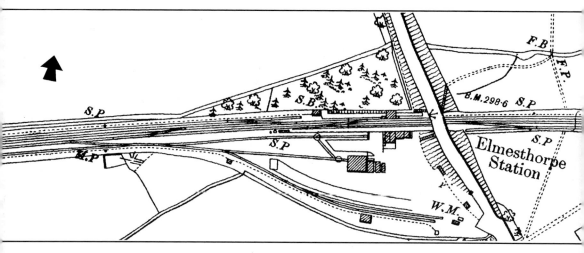

XVIII.   The 1901 revision reveals two wagon turntables to aid loading and unloading. Four flights of steps are shown for the benefit of passengers. Residents numbered 70 in 1901.

48.   This is a view westwards in about 1910. On the right is the start of a long refuge siding and beyond the water tank is the loading gauge. It seems that the goods shed is in poor health and died before the next picture was taken. (P.Laming coll.)

49.   Devoid of a visible driver and displaying a rear lamp, it is clear that the DMU had come **from** Leicester, where the destination had not been changed upon arrival. The date is 1st May 1960. The goods yard would remain in use until 6th April 1964 and the 22-lever signal box was worked until 8th March 1970. (J.S.Gilks/M.J.Stretton)

50.   An eastward photo includes the points of the second refuge siding, together with the staff crossing. Passengers were expected to read the signs on the bridge and walk over it. None were carried after 4th March 1968. (LOSA)

EAST OF ELMESTHORPE

XIX.   The 1946 edition is at 4ins to 1 mile and the quarry system is starting in the granite workings at the bottom. It runs through a curved tunnel and emerges near the church yard, before descending to the exchange sidings, close to the main line. North thereof is a separate system from Barrow Hill Quarry, near Earl Shilton. This village is north of Elmesthorpe.

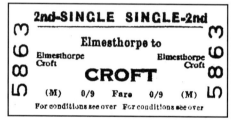

2nd-SINGLE SINGLE-2nd		
Elmesthorpe to		
Elmesthorpe Croft	**CROFT**	Elmesthorpe Croft
(M) 0/9	Fare	0/9 (M)
For conditions see over		For conditions see over

5863   5863

51. Below is *Violet*, Hunslet no. 1146 of 1913. Quarrying ended in 1958 and the pits soon flooded. They were later used to train divers and two wrecked ships were sunk in them. The name became the Underworld Dive Centre. (Unknown)

CROFT

52. Croft Hill was a popular picnic destination for Leicester residents and Sunday Schools, particularly in the 1920s. The peaceful station was photographed in 1952. It was late on the scene, not opening until 1st November 1877. (R.M.Casserley coll.)

53. Well-attended shrubs enhance the scene on 21st September 1961, as a Cravens DMU departs. Later to become class 105, the unit is working the 11.10 from Leicester London Road to Nuneaton Trent Valley. (M.Mensing/M.J.Stretton)

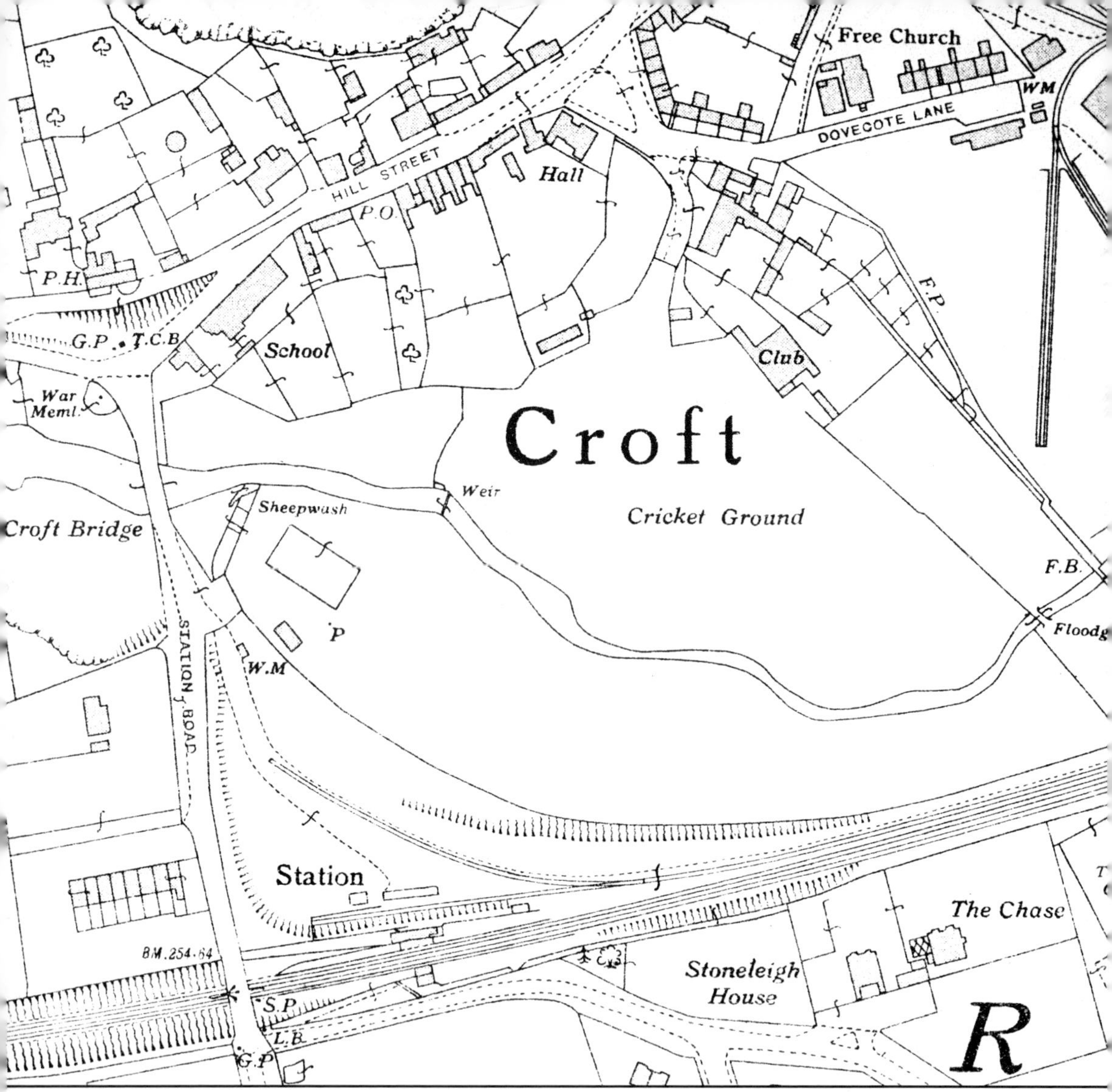

NUNEATON and LEICESTER.—London and North Western.

Miles from Nuneaton	Up.	Week Days.																			Sundays.			
	Lime Street Station,	aft	mrn	mrn	mrn	mrn	k	mrn	mrn		aft	non	f	aft	aft	aft	aft	aft	aft	aft	aft	mrn	mrn	aft
	410 Liverpool ....dep.	....	2 35	....	....	....	....	7 15	9 45		Sats. only.	12 0	....	....	2 40	....	....	5 30	6 15	Sats. only.	....	2 35	9 20	4 5
	410 Manchester †† .. "	....	1155	....	....	....	....	8 30	10 0			1150	12 10	12l55	3 0	....	....	5 30	6 0		y	1155	9 0	4 25
	441 Birmingham ‡‡.. "	....	....	2d50	7 35	....	8 50	1010	11 45			1 3	2 55	4 0	4s5	5e30	....	6 10	7 10		....	8 30	....	5 50
	440 Leamington ‖ .. "	....	....	5 20	8 0	....	9 15	10 5	11 50			1 28	3 2	4 0	4s35	5e45	....	6 50	7 55		....	8 45	....	5 55
	438 Coventry ...... "	....	....	6 25	8 27	....	9 44	11 0	12 28			1 55	3 50	4 32	5s0	6e10	....	7 15	8 20		....	9 45	....	6 30
	402 London (Euston) "	10 0	....	5 0	....	7 10	....	8 35	10c37			1225	1 30	.....	2 45	4 10	5c30	5 35	7e30	8 50	10 0	....	10 0	4 45
—	**Nuneaton** ....dep.	2 15	6 10	7b40	9b0	9 30	10 7	1121	1s5	1 15	1 35	3 0	4 15	5 10	6 0	6 48	7 20	8 30	9 30	1130	2 15	1020	2 15	7 25
4¼	**Hinckley**	mrn	6 19	7 49	9 9	9 39	1016	1130	1s12	1 24	1 44	3 9	4 23	5 18	6 9	7 3	7 27	8 39	9 40	1138	mrn	1029	2 26	7 36
7¼	Elmesthorpe*	....	6 26	7 56	9 16	9 46	....	1137	....	1 31	1 51	3 16	4 30	5 24	6 16	7 9	....	8 46	9 47	1144	....	1036	....	7 43
10	Croft	....	6 32	8 2	9 22	9 52	....	1143	....	1 37	1 57	3 22	4 36	.....	6 22	7 18	....	8 52	9 53	1150	....	1042	2 39	7 51
12	Narborough	....	6 37	8 7	9 27	9 57	....	1148	1s27	1 42	2 2	3 27	4 41	5 35	6 27	7 25	....	8 57	9 58	1155	....	1047	2 45	7 57
13¾	Blaby	....	6 41	8 11	9 31	10 1	....	1152	....	1 46	2 6	3 31	.....	5 39	6 31	7 29	....	9 1	10 2	1159	....	1051	2 49	8 2
15	Wigston (G.P.) [530, 541	....	6 47	8 17	9 37	10 7	....	1158	....	1 52	2 12	3 37	4 47	.....	6 37	7 35	....	9 7	10 9	12 3	....	1057	2 55	8 9
18¾	**Leicester** † 365, 384 arr.	2 52	6 55	8 25	9 46	1015	1035	12 5	1s38	2 2	2 20	3 45	4 55	5 50	6 45	7 42	....	9 17	1020	1210	2 52	11 5	3 5	8 18

Mls	London Road Station,	mrn	mrn	mrn	mrn	n	mrn	aft	aft		aft	aft	aft	aft	n	aft	aft	aft	aft	aft	mrn	mrn	aft	aft
—	**Leicester** (Midland) dep	6 20	.....	8 20	9 2	9 55	1145	1215	1 35	Saturdays only.	2e10	2s42	4 25	5 10	5 52	6 37	8 5	8 55	9 45	10 50	7 55	1130	5 45	9 40
3¾	Wigston (Glen Parva)..	6 30	.....	8 28	9 10	10 3	1153	1224	1 43		2e20	2s51	4 35	5 21	....	6 46	8 14	9 4	9 52	10 58	....	1138	5 53	....
5	Blaby	6 34	.....	8 32	9 14	....	....	1228	1 47		2e24	2s55	4 39	5 25	....	6 50	8 18	9 8	....	11 2	....	1142	5 57	9 48
6¾	Narborough	6 39	.....	8 36	9 18	10 9	1159	1232	1 51		2e28	2s59	4 43	5 29	....	6 54	8 22	9 12	9 57	11 6	8 7	1146	6 2	9 53
8¾	Croft	6 44	.....	8 42	9 24	....	....	1237	1 56		2e33	3s4	4 48	5 34	....	6 59	8 27	9 17	....	11 11	8 12	1151	6 8	....
11½	Elmesthorpe*	6 51	.....	8 49	9 31	1018	12 8	1243	2 3		2e39	3s10	4 54	5 41	....	7 5	8 33	9 23	....	11 18	8 18	1158	6 16	....
14½	**Hinckley** .... [438	6 58	8 30	8 57	9 39	1026	1216	1251	2 11		2e47	3s18	5 2	5 50	6 22	7 13	8 41	9 31	10 9	11 26	8 27	12 6	6 23	10 7
18¾	**Nuneaton** 402, 411, arr.	7 5	8 37	9 5	9 47	1041	1230	1 2	2 20		2e59	3s26	5 10	6 0	6 30	7 22	8 50	9 40	1018	11 35	8 35	1215	6 34	1016
115¾	411 **London** (Eustn) arr.	9 55	10a50	1125	1225	1 5	3 15	5 15	5 15		5e40	6s10	8 10	....	....	1045	‡	....	....	5 50	....	4 20	9 0	....
28¾	438 Coventry .. ... "	8h14	.....	9 48	1022	11 3	....	1 30	....		3e47	3s57	5 45	....	6 54	8 48	9 31	....	....	....	9 13	....	7 51	....
38¼	441 Leamington ‖ .. "	8 55	.....	....	1050	1130	....	1 56	....		4e15	4s24	6 10	....	7 22	9 15	1019	....	....	....	10 5	....	8 20	....
47¾	440 Birmingham ‡‡.. "	9n14	.....	1030	1130	12 8	....	2f22	....		4e45	4s45	7 2	....	8 10	9 39	1040	....	....	....	1020	....	10 0	....
110½	403 Manchester †† .. "	10 0	.....	12 5	1 30	....	3 5	4 34	5 27		6e5	6s5	8 15	....	....	1035	1t10	....	....	2 58	....	3 55	9 42	2 58
114	403 Liverpool (L.St.) "	1025	.....	1210	1 35	....	3 10	5 8	5 8		6e30	6s30	8 50	....	....	1040	1240	t	....	3 10	....	4 5	9 55	3 10

a Arrives at 11 10 mrn. on Mons.
b Call at **Welford Road**, Leicester, on Weds. and Sats. to set down.
c By slip carriage.
d Leaves at 5 35 mrn. on Mondays.
e Except Saturdays.
f Through Train, Coventry to Nottingham (Mid.), see pages 438 and 534.
g Saturday night.
h Arrives 7 33 mrn. on Mondays.
i Arrives at 2 30 aft. on Saturdays.
k Through Train from Leamington to Nottingham (Mid.), see pages 440, 438, and 532.
l Leaves at 12 40 aft. on Saturdays.
n Through Trains from Nottingham (Mid.) to Leamington, see pages 541, 545, 438, and 441 respectively.
n Arrives 8 39 mrn. on Mondays.
s Saturdays only.
t Except Sunday mornings.
* Station for Barwell (2¼ miles) and Earl Shilton (1¾ miles).
† Midland Station (London Road).
‡ 1st and 3rd class.
‖ Avenue Station.
†† London Road Station.
‡‡ New Street Station.

March 1909

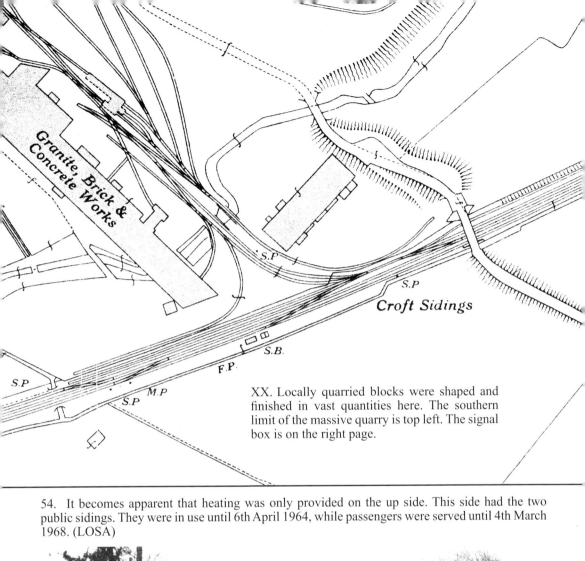

Granite, Brick & Concrete Works

S.P

S.P

Croft Sidings

S.B.

F.P.

S.P

M.P

S.P

XX. Locally quarried blocks were shaped and finished in vast quantities here. The southern limit of the massive quarry is top left. The signal box is on the right page.

54. It becomes apparent that heating was only provided on the up side. This side had the two public sidings. They were in use until 6th April 1964, while passengers were served until 4th March 1968. (LOSA)

CROFT

EAST OF CROFT

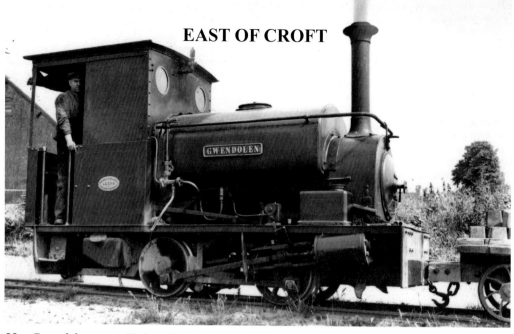

55. *Gwendolen* was a Hudswell Clarke 0-4-0ST. It was used here from new in 1921 until 1949, when it was scrapped. The 3ft 1½ ins gauge system was on the north side of the works shown on the map. (A.Neale coll.)

56. Aggregate Industries became the operator of the plant, which is seen on 14th April 1984. Its regional offices are in the village. No. 31415 is heading a Birmingham to Norwich service. The 1901 box had 30 levers and was called Croft Sidings until 31st July 2006, when it was fitted with a workstation. Then, it was simply "Croft", until closure on 2nd January 2012. (P.D.Shannon)

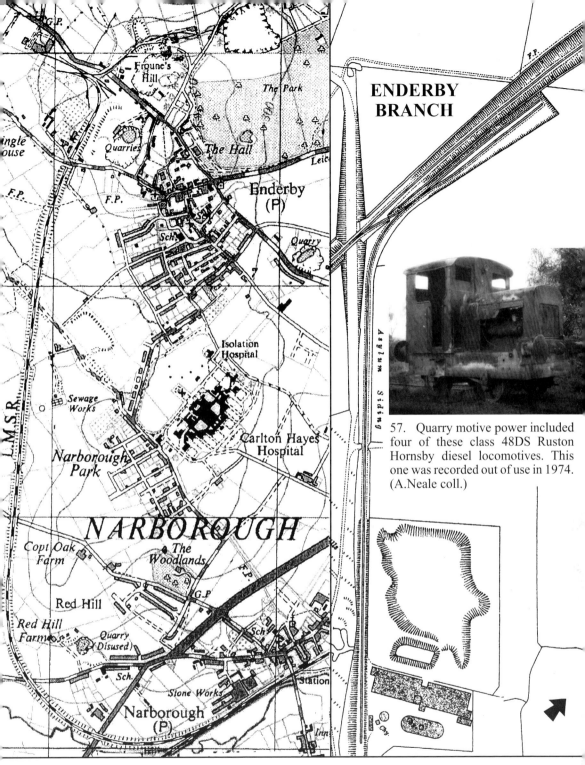

ENDERBY BRANCH

57. Quarry motive power included four of these class 48DS Ruston Hornsby diesel locomotives. This one was recorded out of use in 1974. (A.Neale coll.)

XXI.   There were three massive granite quarries at the end of the 1912 single line branch, which is shown to terminate on the curve at the top of this 1938 map, which is printed at 4ins to 1 mile. They have largely been infilled with refuse, but part of one is used for climbing. A brickworks siding was opened north of the Sewage Works, initially serving the hospital, as seen on the right map, which is from 1914 and is at 20ins to 1 mile. The entire branch was in use to the northern curve by 1901. A boot and shoe factory had opened in 1888 in Enderby. Total closure came in 1980.

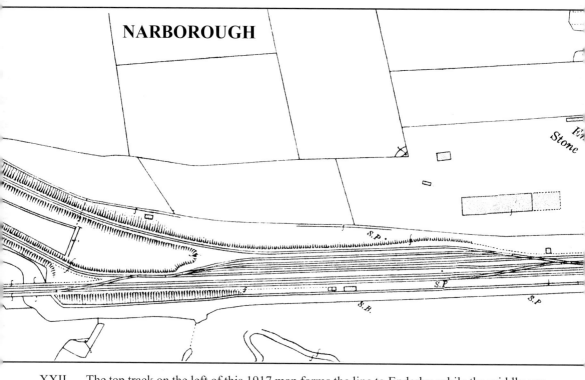

NARBOROUGH

XXII.   The top track on the left of this 1917 map forms the line to Enderby, while the middle one is the headshunt for the exchange sidings. It is evident that the River Soar had been straightened to align with the railway, closely.

XXIII.   At a smaller scale, the same edition reveals overhead and narrow gauge transport systems serving two small quarries on the fringe of the granite outcrop. In places it is formed of vertical columns of stone, as in the Giant's Causeway.

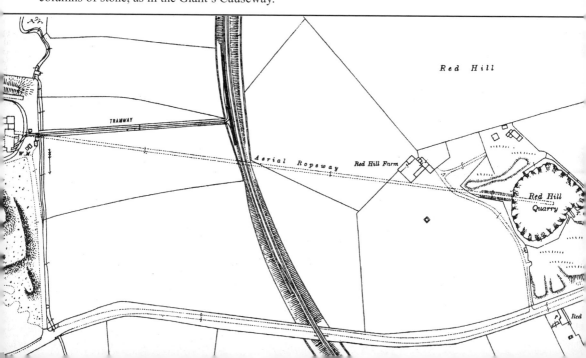

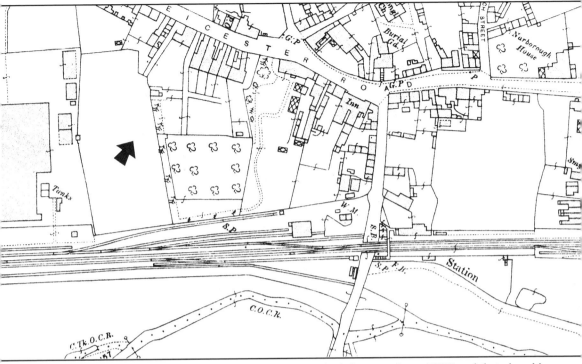

58.   An early postcard shows No. 2 Box. No. 1 is on the left page of map XXII and that closed in 1952. No. 2 opened in 1875 and it had a 23-lever frame, until a panel came in 1986. After closure on 31st July 2006, it became a Listed Building. (P.Laming coll.)

59. An eastbound train approaches on 4th October 1952 and passes the Empire Stone Works. The changes of station roof line suggest a number of alterations over the years. The population grew from 902 in 1901 to 8402 in 1961. (R.Humm coll.)

60. The station approach was recorded on 3rd August 1985. The goods yard was in use until 1st August 1966. The station closed to passengers on 4th March 1968, but support from Blaby Council brought its reopening on 5th January 1970. (N.D.Mundy)

61.   This panorama from the footbridge is from 1986, while a Birmingham New Street to Leicester service arrives. Just one siding remained behind the train, but there were still four listed in 1990. These DMUs were produced in York Works from 1985 onwards; this is no. 150113. (J.Whitehouse)

62.   No. 66131 is passing the barriers on 16th June 2004, while passengers wait on both of the new platforms. A basic hourly service was on offer by that time. The class 66 was a General Motors creation, produced from 1998. (M.J.Stretton)

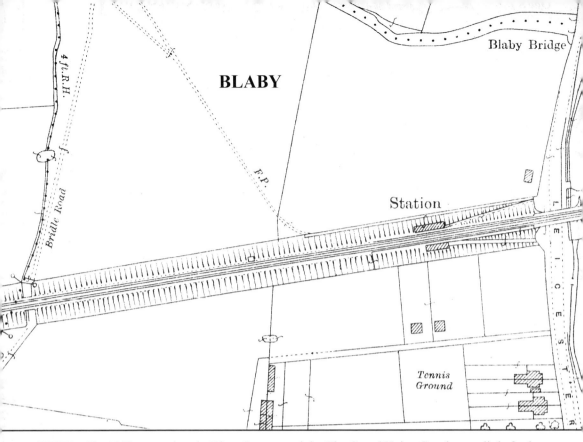

BLABY

Blaby Bridge

Station

Bridle Road

F.P.

4 ft. R.H.

Tennis Ground

L E I C E S T E R

XXIV.   The 1930 survey has the River Sence top right. The Grand Union Canal was a little further north and a chemical works was on its north bank.

63.   The north side is seen on 12th July 1914 following protest action by ladies of the Suffragette Movement. There was water nearby (right) for the fire brigade. (P.Laming coll.)

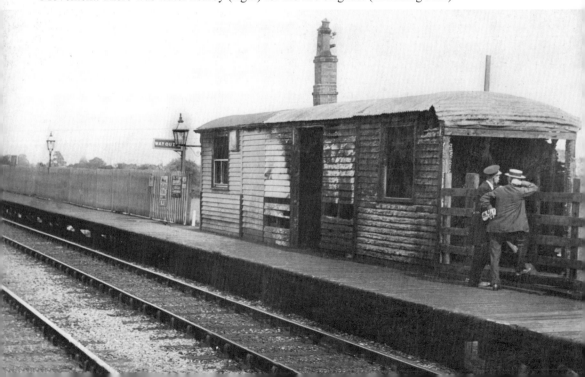

XXV.   The 1946 edition at 1in to 1 mile reveals the proximity of the village, which housed 1842 in 1901 and 4242 in 1961. The three stations on the right are worthy of study at this stage. The GCR is north-south on the left. A linking curve had been built in the northeast quadrant. See caption 37 in the Middleton Press album, *Rugby to Loughborough*.

64.   A fine panorama on the south side was recorded on an undated postcard. The need for step-free access was included on the right. (P.Laming coll.)

65.   Entirely of timber construction, the station opened on 1st November 1864. It is seen not long before closure on 4th March 1968. (SLS coll.)

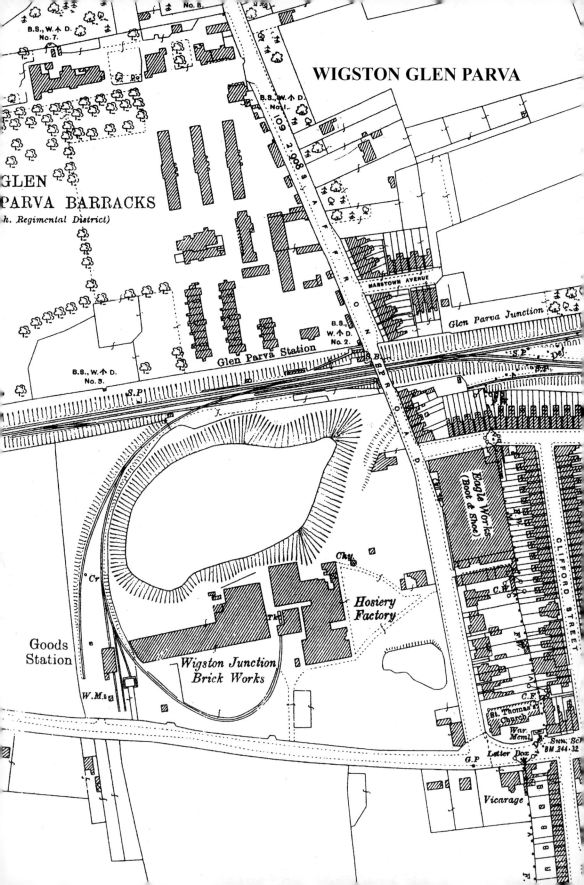

WIGSTON GLEN PARVA

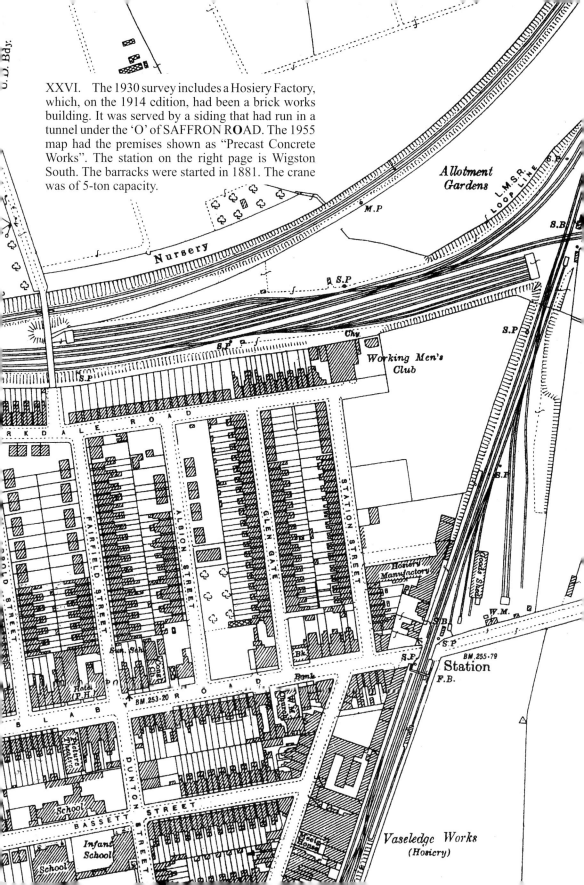

XXVI.   The 1930 survey includes a Hosiery Factory, which, on the 1914 cdition, had been a brick works building. It was served by a siding that had run in a tunnel under the 'O' of SAFFRON ROAD. The 1955 map had the premises shown as "Precast Concrete Works". The station on the right page is Wigston South. The barracks were started in 1881. The crane was of 5-ton capacity.

O.D. Bdy.

Allotment Gardens

L.M.S.R. LOOP LINE

S.B.

M.P

S.B.

Nursery

S.P

S.P

Chy.

Working Men's Club

S.P

S.P

RKDALE ROAD

FAIRFIELD STREET

ALBON STREET

GLEN GATE

STATION STREET

Hosiery Manufactory

S.P

W.M.

S.B.

S.P

BLABY ROAD

Sun. Sch.

Hotel (P.H.)

BM.253.20

Bank

Bk.

S.P

Station
F.B.

BM.255.79

DUNTON STREET

Picture Theatre

School

Infant School

School

BASSETT STREET

Week Homes

Vaseledge Works
(Hosiery)

66.   The station opened to passengers on 1st April 1884, as just GLEN PARVA. It had opened earlier to serve the barracks. The prefix was added in 1887. The station is near the centre of the left page of the map. (P.Laming coll.)

67.   Glen Parva Junction is visible through the arch and on the right are the down side buildings. Above the roof of the right one is the start of the steep steps down to the platform. The high fence would catch those who fall. (R.Humm coll.)

68. Gas lights and junction signals are worthy of study in this unusual composition. Even the conker is missing. The gate controlled access to the dock, at which the van is standing in the next picture. (R.Humm coll.)

69. Passing through on 27th April 1948 is no. 45320, a class 5 4-6-0. It is hauling the 5.45pm from Leicester to Birmingham. The goods yard would close on 4th July 1966. (W.A.Camwell/SLS)

70. Glen Parva Junction was the name used for the 24-lever box, which was in use until 23rd July 1973. The station closed on 4th March 1968 and was photographed on 5th May 1968, as the 15.10 Leicester to Birmingham ran through. The building on the left had been enlarged in 1904 to make provision for a waiting room for ladies. (M.Mitchell/M/J.Stretton)

SOUTH WIGSTON

71. This class 31-hauled Birmingham-Norwich train has just run under Saffron Road, early in 1986. This is on the left page of the last map. It is viewed from the narrow bridge on the facing page, while the new station was under construction. (J.Whitehouse)

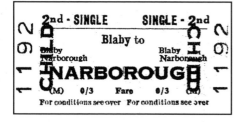

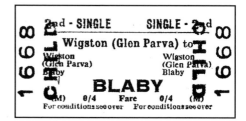

72. The new station opened on 12th May 1986 and is seen from the same viewpoint on 12th October 1988. Sprinter no. 150114 is working from Coventry to Nottingham. (H.A.Gamble)

73. The platforms are staggered, with one each side of the footbridge, but no car park was provided. No. 150148 is also running a service from Coventry, but one week later. (H.A.Gamble)

NORTH OF SOUTH WIGSTON

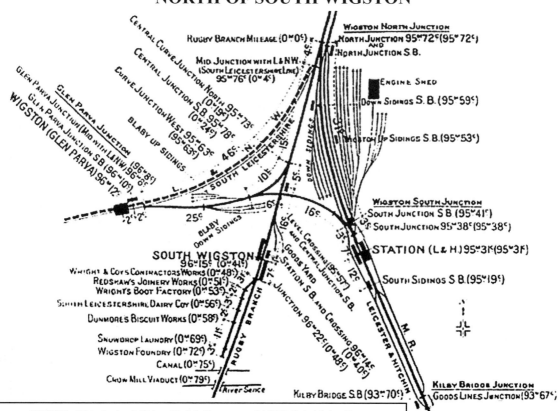

Diagram labels (MR official diagram of 1905):

RUGBY BRANCH MILEAGE (0ᴹ0ᶜ)
CENTRAL CURVE JUNCTION
CENTRAL CURVE JUNCTION NORTH
MID JUNCTION WITH L&NW. (SOUTH LEICESTERSHIRE LINE) 95ᴹ76ᶜ (0ᴹ4ᶜ)
CENTRAL JUNCTION (0ᴹ19ᶜ)
CURVE JUNCTION S.B. 95ᴹ73ᶜ
CURVE JUNCTION WEST 95ᴹ78ᶜ (0ᴹ24ᶜ)
BLABY UP SIDINGS
GLEN PARVA JUNCTION
GLEN PARVA JUNCTION S.B.
GLEN PARVA JUNCTION (MID WITH L&NW) 96ᴹ8ᶜ
GLEN PARVA JUNCTION S.B. (96ᴹ6ᶜ)
WIGSTON (GLEN PARVA) 96ᴹ12ᶜ
WIGSTON NORTH JUNCTION
NORTH JUNCTION 95ᴹ72ᶜ (95ᴹ72ᶜ) AND NORTH JUNCTION S.B.
ENGINE SHED
DOWN SIDINGS S.B. (95ᴹ59ᶜ)
WIGSTON UP SIDINGS S.B. (95ᴹ53ᶜ)
SOUTH LEICESTERSHIRE
WIGSTON SOUTH JUNCTION
SOUTH JUNCTION S.B. (95ᴹ41ᶜ)
SOUTH JUNCTION 95ᴹ38ᶜ (95ᴹ38ᶜ)
STATION (L&H.) 95ᴹ3ᴷ (95ᴹ3ꜰ)
SOUTH SIDINGS S.B. (95ᴹ19ᶜ)
SOUTH WIGSTON 96ᴹ15ᶜ (0ᴹ41ᶜ)
WRIGHT & COYS CONTRACTORS WORKS (0ᴹ48ᶜ)
REDSHAW'S JOINERY WORKS (0ᴹ51ᶜ)
WRIGHTS BOOT FACTORY (0ᴹ53ᶜ)
SOUTH LEICESTERSHIRE DAIRY COY (0ᴹ56ᶜ)
DUNMORES BISCUIT WORKS (0ᴹ58ᶜ)
SNOWDROP LAUNDRY (0ᴹ69ᶜ)
WIGSTON FOUNDRY (0ᴹ72ᶜ)
CANAL (0ᴹ75ᶜ)
CROW MILL VIADUCT (0ᴹ79ᶜ)
RIVER SENCE
LEVEL CROSSING (96ᴹ57ᶜ) AND CENTRAL JUNCTION
GOODS YARD
STATION S.B.
JUNCTION S.B. AND CROSSING
JUNCTION 96ᴹ22ᶜ (0ᴹ48ᶜ) (0ᴹ40ᶜ)
RUGBY BRANCH
KILBY BRIDGE S.B. (93ᴹ70ᶜ)
KILBY BRIDGE JUNCTION
GOODS LINES JUNCTION (93ᴹ67ᶜ)
LEICESTER & HITCHIN
M.R.

XXVII. This is the MR's official diagram of 1905. It laid the line across the map in 1872 to enable it to run through coaches between St. Pancras and Birmingham via Kettering. The centre line is shown as RUGBY BRANCH; we will cover this from picture 94 onwards. The views herein to 83 cover the area within the triangle, randomly. The station on the right is illustrated in pictures 59 to 63 in our *Wellingborough to Leicester* album.

74. We are on the bridge used for pictures 71-73 in May 1963, looking east. Class 4F 0-6-0 no. 44030 is shunting Blaby Sidings. (M.Mitchell/M.J.Stretton)

75. Wigston Central Box is in the left background of the previous picture and this shows the crossing of the two routes on the level. The view is from August 1962 and includes the former MR engine shed in the distance. The box had 32 levers. (R.Humm coll.)

76. The MR shed was visited on 5th November 1934, soon after it had closed for regular use. Two steam railcars are resting alongside no. 3420. The building was subsequently used as a workshop for stock repairs until 1955. (H.N.James/R.Humm)

77. Crowds are out to witness the passing of the Royal Train. Both signals are 'off' and both lavatory windows are evident. The postcard producer offered no details. The box is Wigston South Junction. (P.Laming coll.)

78. Passing Wigston South Junction on 1st August 1958 are nos. 44123 and 46400, while working from Clacton to Birmingham. The former was an ex-LMS class 4F and the latter an ex-LMS class 2 2-6-0; the stock was very varied. The water column has its own heater nearby.
(M.J.Stretton coll.)

79. "Jubilee" class 4-6-0 no. 45649 *Hawkins* hauled a 1961 Cup Final Special for Tottenham Hotspur vs. Leicester City; the score was 2-0 to Spurs. It ran from Hinckley to St Pancras and is passing Wigston South Junction on 6th May 1961. The box was in use from 1900 to 1986.
(R.Humm coll.)

80. The Advanced Passenger Train is on a rarely seen test run; it never went into production. It eventually went on show at Crewe Heritage Centre. The train has just passed Wigston South Junction in May 1977 and has been subjected to Advanced Camera Systems - the telephoto lens. Such distortions seldom appear in Middleton Press albums.
(R.Thwaites/M.J.Stretton)

81. We are at Wigston North Junction, where we see its 20-lever box and a severe speed restriction on 12th April 1969. Staff transport and means of point heating are on show. (M.A.King/R.Humm)

SOUTH OF LEICESTER

82. Almost two miles north of the last junction was Knighton North Junction, where the MR branched west to Burton-on-Trent. This box had 20 levers, while South Junction Box had 60. The line from there was still in use for freight in 2016. "Jubilee" class no. 45599 *Bechuanaland* is working from Nuneaton on 11th June 1963. (H.A.Gamble/R.Humm)

83. Emerging from the south end of Knighton Tunnel is a class 2F "Cauliflower" 0-6-0. The tunnel is 104yds in length and the north portal is one mile from Leicester station. The western tunnel was the second one to be completed. (R.M.Casserley coll.)

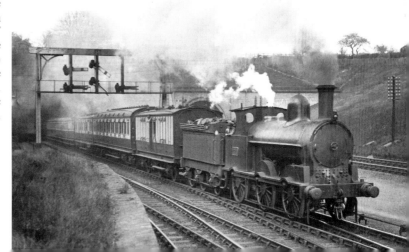

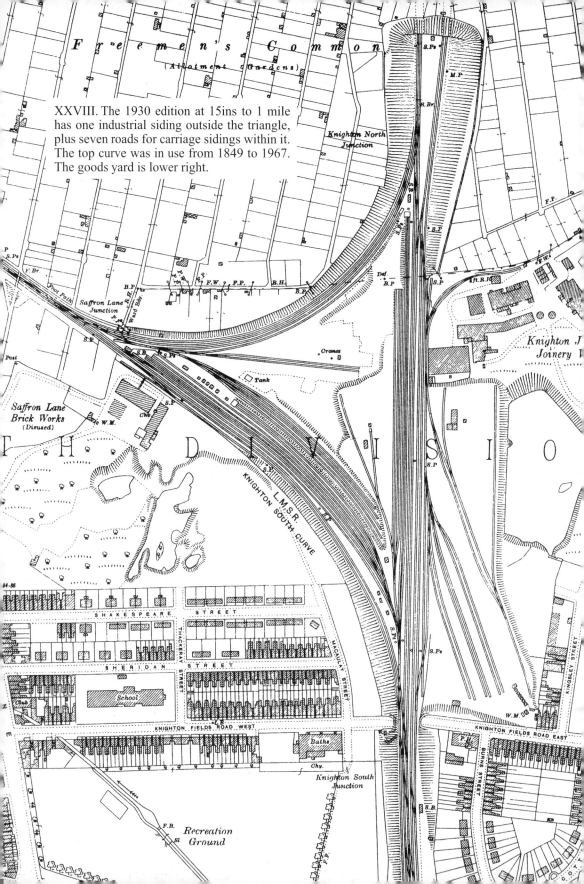

XXVIII. The 1930 edition at 15ins to 1 mile has one industrial siding outside the triangle, plus seven roads for carriage sidings within it. The top curve was in use from 1849 to 1967. The goods yard is lower right.

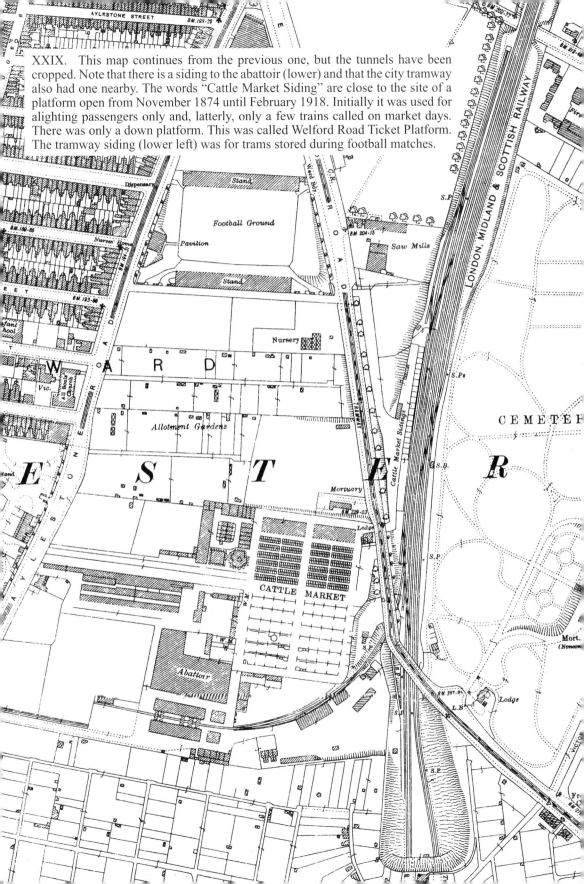

XXIX. This map continues from the previous one, but the tunnels have been cropped. Note that there is a siding to the abattoir (lower) and that the city tramway also had one nearby. The words "Cattle Market Siding" are close to the site of a platform open from November 1874 until February 1918. Initially it was used for alighting passengers only and, latterly, only a few trains called on market days. There was only a down platform. This was called Welford Road Ticket Platform. The tramway siding (lower left) was for trams stored during football matches.

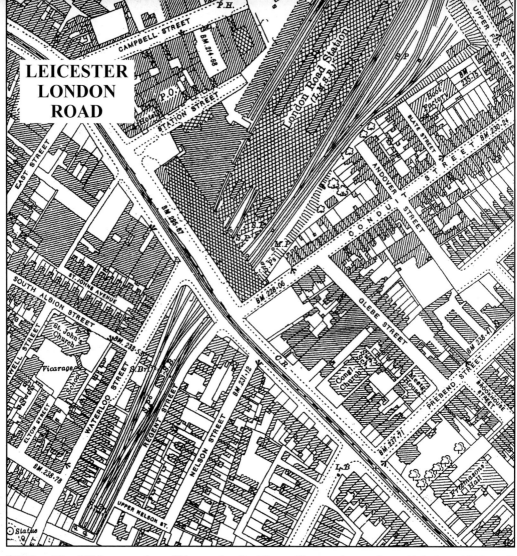

LEICESTER
LONDON
ROAD

XXX. The 1930 survey is at 20ins to 1 mile. The suffix was in use from 12th June 1892 until 4th May 1969. The engine shed was beyond the top border.

84. The first station was approached via Campbell Street, which is at the top of the map. The exit was later in Station Street. The fine elevation seen here in 1912 was completed by the MR in 1892. The frontage was finished in 1894. Electric trams ran from 1904 to 1949. (P.Laming coll.)

85. The new station was completed in the early 1890s, with full roofing and modern smoke ducting. The footbridges could then be used without coughing or having to wash. (LOSA)

86. The Nazi bombing of World War II meant that the glazing was lost or had to be removed for safety reasons. Seen on 22nd May 1965 is "Jubilee" class 4-6-0 no. 45660 *Rooke*, with a terminated train. (P.J.Shoesmith/J.Whitehouse)

LEICESTER

87. The suffix was changed to Midland on 5th May 1969, but not used after 4th May 1970. It is 19th April 1975 and a class 120 DMU has terminated and stands on a siding, which had connections at both ends. (F.Hornby)

88. Having been cleaned up after the war, the exterior looks tidy in April 1987, but the interior had been converted to a car park at its south end. (M.J.Stretton)

89.   The remains of the extensive roof framework were removed in 1975 and two island platforms were created, devoid of through lines. It is 4th February 1995 and we see the 14.20 Coventry to Newark Castle waiting to depart. (M.J.Stretton)

90.   The platform roofing and lighting can be examined more closely on 22nd May 1996. The dock and the three sidings were later removed. No. 156417 is working the 15.12 Coventry to Sleaford. It will soon pass the diesel depot. (M.J.Stretton)

91. Diverted away from London because of weekend engineering work, no. 66414 heads south through Leicester with the 10.32 Felixstowe North to Birmingham Lawley Street Freightliner train on 23rd August 2014. It will continue its journey via Hinckley and Nuneaton. A 'Meridian' unit enters the station on a down service from London St. Pancras. In the centre had been London Road Junction box. It had 50 levers and was in use from 20th December 1935 until 29th June 1986. (P.D.Shannon)

For other views of Leicester stations, see
Wellingborough to Leicester, Leicester to Burton
and *Rugby to Loughborough* **albums.**

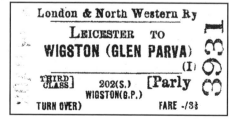

London & North Western Ry
LEICESTER TO
WIGSTON (GLEN PARVA)
(I)
THIRD CLASS] 202(S.) [Parly
WIGSTON(G.P.)
TURN OVER) FARE -/3½
3931

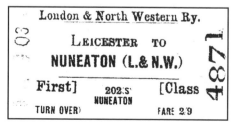

London & North Western Ry.
03
LEICESTER TO
NUNEATON (L.& N.W.)
First] 202 S. [Class
NUNEATON
TURN OVER) FARE 2 9
4871

92. The northern arch is seen on 21st July 2015. The original clock tower can also be appreciated, as can the alterations within, at this end. The clock was reported to be the last on a station to be hand wound. (V.Mitchell)

93. Seen on 31st March 2016, the interior of the porte-cochere has the eastern end given over to taxis. Beyond the screen is the station entrance to the right, and the rear of the DEPARTURE arches to the left. The up island platform was provided with a 1st class lounge in 2000 and automatic ticket barriers arrived in 2006. (A.C.Hartless)

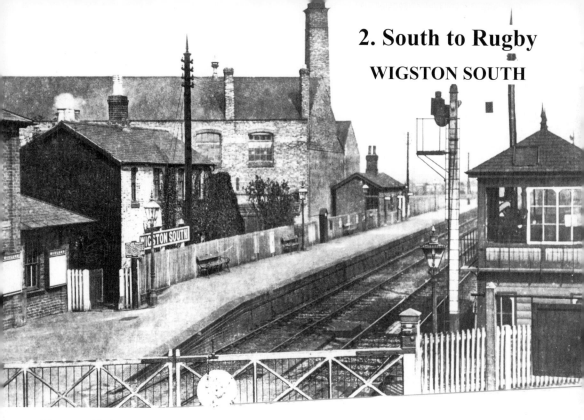

94. For this location, please see map XXVI (lower right), near picture 66. We are looking north from the footbridge, with MIDLAND headings on the timetable boards. The suffix SOUTH was added on 1st October 1868. (LOSA)

95. The other platform is seen in 1952 and a hedge has grown up. It was south of the level crossing. The yard closed on 2nd May 1966. (R.Humm coll.)

96.   The 4.50pm Leicester to Rugby is arriving behind class 4 2-6-4T no. 42062 on 27th June 1959. The 20-lever signal box dated from 1890. The main building housed the station master and his family, plus the booking office. (M.Mensing/M.J.Stretton)

97.   The white painted building contained staff cottages. Passenger traffic ceased on 1st January 1962. The photo was taken on 8th March 1961. (A.Swain/M.J.Stretton)

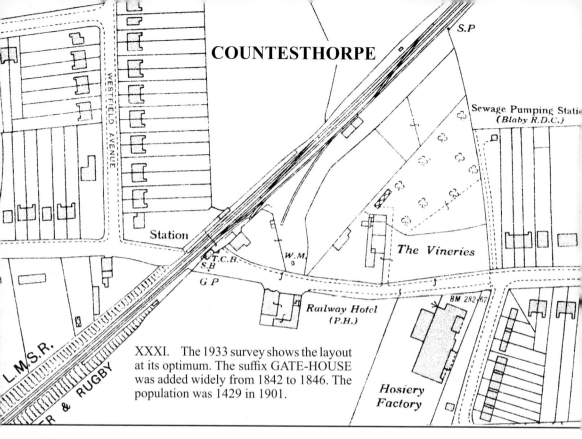

COUNTESTHORPE

S.P

Sewage Pumping Stati
(Blaby R.D.C.)

Station

The Vineries

T.C.B.
S.B
W.M.

G P

Railway Hotel
(P.H.)

BM 282·67

L.M.S.R.

R & RUGBY

Hosiery
Factory

XXXI.   The 1933 survey shows the layout
at its optimum. The suffix GATE-HOUSE
was added widely from 1842 to 1846. The
population was 1429 in 1901.

98.   The earliest evidence of a train stopping here is in August 1841, with one on Saturdays. By 1st March 1844, there was also one on Wednesdays. From March 1846, there was a full service. The low platform was for parcel traffic. (P.Laming coll.)

99. The single gate was worked by the signalman on foot. At least he had generous gas lighting and a good road surface. (P.Laming coll.)

100. The other passenger platform is featured here. Local passengers were requested to travel in the rear coaches of the train. This panorama is from 4th October 1952. (R.Humm coll.)

101. The signal box had 16 levers and closed on 1st January 1962, when all service ceased. Both platforms retain their white limewash edging, introduced during the blackout of World War II. (SLS coll.)

102. Doorless and roofless, the cast iron urinal was at least decorative and functional. This is seen five months after retirement. One is still in use on Bewdley station on the Severn Valley Railway. (M.J.Stretton)

103. The Leicestershire Railway Society ran this special train on the final day of full operation, 30th December 1961. No. 42331 was a class 4 2-6-4T of LMS origin and its shed plate shows 15C. This means that it was based at Leicester Midland shed. (H.Gamble/M.J.Stretton)

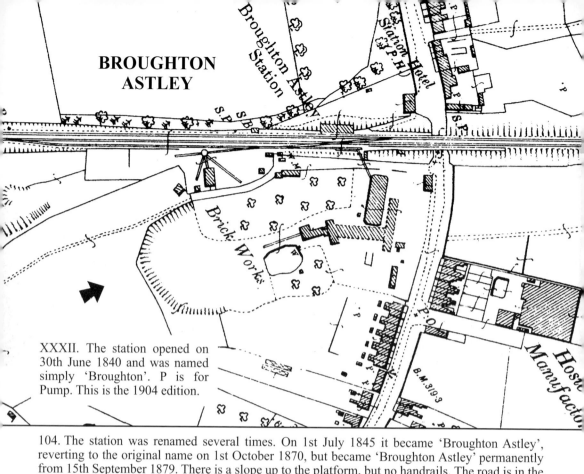

BROUGHTON ASTLEY

XXXII. The station opened on 30th June 1840 and was named simply 'Broughton'. P is for Pump. This is the 1904 edition.

104. The station was renamed several times. On 1st July 1845 it became 'Broughton Astley', reverting to the original name on 1st October 1870, but became 'Broughton Astley' permanently from 15th September 1879. There is a slope up to the platform, but no handrails. The road is in the foreground. (LOSA)

105. The signal box was to the left of the cameraman. The train has been moved to the wrong line, to allow for another one to pass. Residents numbered 1172 in 1901. The box had 16 levers and closed with the line. (P.Laming coll.)

106. The platform has had its extension removed and its building changed by the time this photo was taken in 1952. ASTLEY was often omitted until 1879 and was sometimes hyphenated earlier. (R.M.Casserley coll.)

107. A mixed train rattles through on 9th July 1960, hauled by class 8F 2-8-0 no. 48370. This class was introduced by the LMS in 1935 and was immensely successful. 666 were in use at one time on BR in the 1950s. (H.B.Priestley/R.Humm)

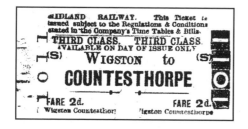

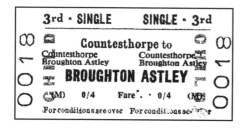

LEIRE HALT

108. The halt opened on 2nd March 1925 and was closed with the line. The guard was required to attend to the paraffin lamps. (D.K.Jones coll.)

XXXIII. The halt is near the centre of this extract from the 1946 map at 1in to 1 mile. The adjacent stations are included. The ex-GCR route is on the right.

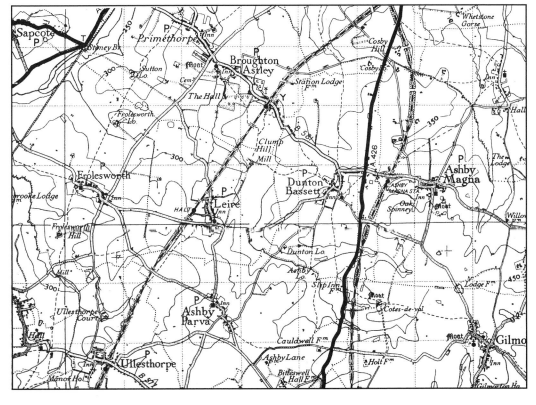

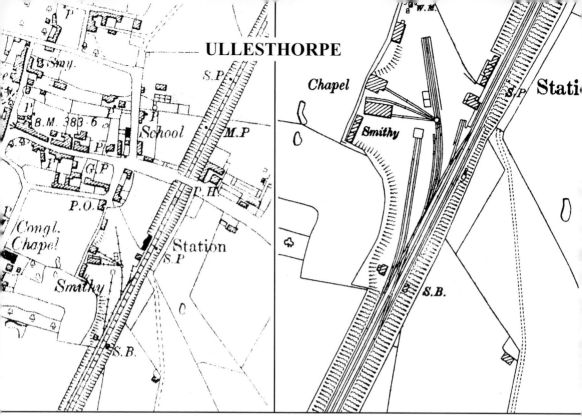

ULLESTHORPE

XXXIV. The 1904 survey is shown at 12½ ins to 1 mile, on the left. Residents numbered 312 in the 1901 census. One chapel and two smithies sufficed. On the right is the same edition at double the scale.

109. In the distance is the 16-lever signal box, which closed with the line on 1st January 1962. The station opened as just 'Ullesthorpe' on 30th June 1840. It became 'Ullesthorpe for Lutterworth' on 1st May 1879. From 1st August 1897, it was 'Ullesthorpe and Lutterworth'. (LOSA)

110. From 1st February 1930, the name was just 'Ullesthorpe'. This is a 1951 view, which records the luxurious styling of the house for the station master to reflect his status. (R.M.Casserley coll.)

111. His assistant had similar fine windows. The crane here was horse-drawn, as late as 1952. Two miles to the south was Willey Crossing, which had an 8-lever box until line closure. The line crossed the A5 Watling Street here. It was a block post from 1935. (R.M.Casserley coll.)

WEST OF RUGBY

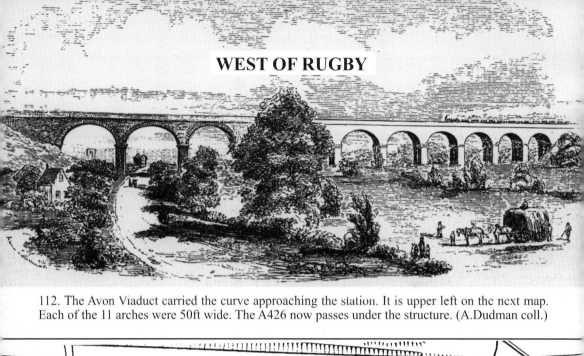

112. The Avon Viaduct carried the curve approaching the station. It is upper left on the next map. Each of the 11 arches were 50ft wide. The A426 now passes under the structure. (A.Dudman coll.)

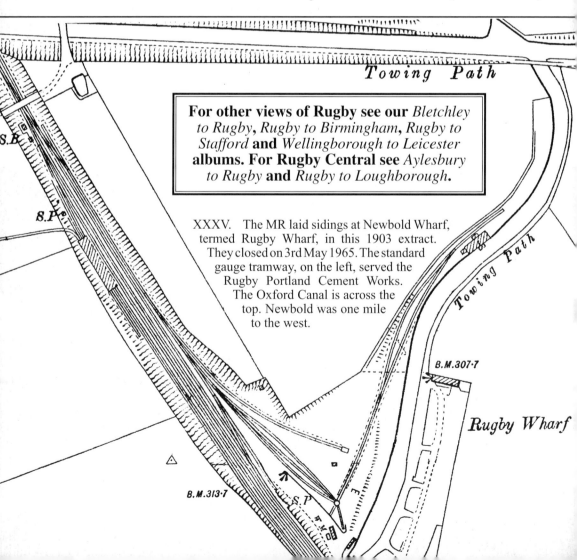

Towing Path

For other views of Rugby see our *Bletchley to Rugby,* **Rugby to Birmingham,** *Rugby to Stafford* **and** *Wellingborough to Leicester* **albums. For Rugby Central see** *Aylesbury to Rugby* **and** *Rugby to Loughborough.*

XXXV. The MR laid sidings at Newbold Wharf, termed Rugby Wharf, in this 1903 extract. They closed on 3rd May 1965. The standard gauge tramway, on the left, served the Rugby Portland Cement Works. The Oxford Canal is across the top. Newbold was one mile to the west.

Towing Path

S.B.

S.P.

B.M.307·7

Rugby Wharf

B.M.313·7

RUGBY

113. We look southeast in this fine panorama from October 1934. Horse-drawn parcel service was still in use. On the left is No. 5 Box. The goods depot closed in 1965. From 1939 to 1964, the number of levers was thus: 161 in No. 1, 32 in No. 2, 28 in No. 3, 90 in No. 4, 173 in No. 5 and 135 in No. 7. No. 6 had closed in 1939. (R.Humm coll.)

114. It is 1954 and we see one of the four bays, right (No. 3). The station had the suffix MIDLAND from 29th May 1950 until 4th May 1970, just after the Eastern Region (ex-LNER) line had closed. It had become part of the London Midland Region in 1958. (Stations UK)

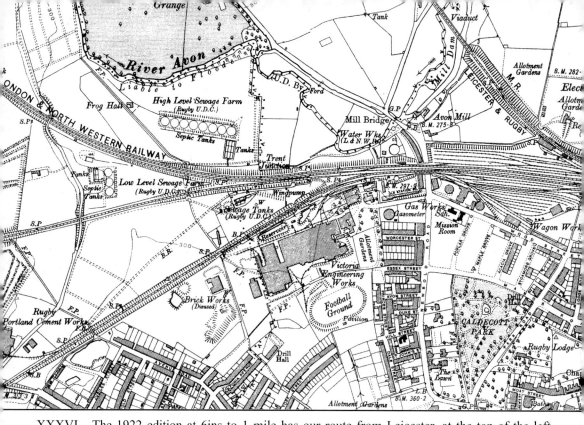

XXXVI. The 1922 edition at 6ins to 1 mile has our route from Leicester, at the top of the left page, and the GCR, almost vertical on the right page. For the first two years, trains from Leicester terminated at the north end of Railway Terrace. The L&BR station was then near Newbold Road. The MR part of the station remained in use until 8th March 1930. The 12-road engine shed was coded 2A and closed in 1965. The two separate small stations were replaced by one in 1851. The station on the right page and in the photos was started in 1885. The MR's direct route to London from Leicester opened in 1858 and its Rugby line then became a branch. BR's Testing Station for locomotives was situated lower right in 1948-59.

115. We move to about 1961 and No. 2 Box comes into view, from Platform 1. On the 'Down Through' is a class 8F 2-8-0, on the scissors crossing. The side glazing was steadily reduced all round. (Stations UK)

116. We move to the north end of Platform 1, still in 1961. Bays numbered 5 and 6 were operational and one could still enjoy studying the diversity of parcels in transit by passenger train. On the left is a tail lamp and corridor end panel, idle since two trains had just been connected. (Stations UK)

117. Arriving at platform 6 on 27th December 1961 is a DMU still bearing its original 'Cats Whiskers'. It is arriving in the Leicester bay. AEI refers to Associated Electrical Industries. The first batch of colour light signals here came into use in 1939. (P.Kingston)

118. Moving back to near the viewpoint of picture 114, we can enjoy more details in this 1964 photograph. The complex station roof lasted until 2000, when platform canopies arrived. The main upgrades took place in 2006-08. (Stations UK)

119. It is 31st May 1990 and little had changed since steam days. Overhead electrification northwards had come into use on 16th November 1964 and south to Euston on 18th April 1966. A multi-storey car park was completed in 2010 and annual station usage had exceeded 2 million by 2015. Rugby Power Signal Box served the area from 14th September 1964 to 3rd June 2012, and Rugby Signalling Control Centre did so subsequently. This had opened on 7th June 2004 to serve northern areas. The former was north of the station and the latter to the south of it. (M.J.Stretton)

120. A new down platform was opened on the through line on the left on 29th May 2007. It was numbered 1, with the old No. 1 becoming 2 and the northern ones 4, 5 and 6. The No. 3 was given to old No. 6 and the other bays taken out of use. No. 31514 is proceeding north on 19th September 1993, while a postal trolley waits for retirement day. The old refreshment room on platforms 2 and 3 was converted into a large cycle storage area, with fitted racks, in 2016. (M.J.Stretton)

Middleton Press

EVOLVING THE ULTIMATE RAIL **ENCYCLOPEDIA**

Easebourne Midhurst GU29 9AZ. Tel:01730 813169

www.middletonpress.co.uk   email:info@middletonpress.co.uk

A-978 0 906520   B- 978 1 873793   C-978 1 901706   D-978 1 904474
E- 978 1 906008   F - 978 1 908174   G - 978 1 910356